GROWING SEASONS

GROWING SEASONS

HEARTFELT RECIPES, DIY STYLE AND DÉCOR,
AND INSPIRATION TO HELP YOU FIND
BEAUTY AND WONDER IN EACH DAY

KRISTIN JOHNS

HARPERONE
An Imprint of HarperCollins*Publishers*

HarperCollins books may be purchased for educational, business, or
sales promotional use. For information, please email the Special Markets
Department at SPsales@harpercollins.com.

FIRST EDITION

Designed by Janet Evans-Scanlon

Unless otherwise noted, photographs provided by Jonathan Volk.
Photographs on p. viii, 6, 12, 49, 53, 63, 69, 72, 102, 105, 120, 188
provided by Hannah Wesby. Photographs on p. 92, 97, 144 provided
by Pauline Falik.

Illustrations on p. 8–9, 26–27, 42–43, 60–62, 74–76, 94–96, 112–14,
130–32, 146–48, 164–65, 180–82, 198–200 copyright
© JOJOSTUDIO/Shutterstock.

Library of Congress Cataloging-in-Publication Data has been applied for.

ISBN 978-0-06-321573-3

23 24 25 26 27 TC 10 9 8 7 6 5 4 3 2 1

*To my mom and dad who have raised me
with unconditional love and support,
and to Marcus and James who are
my whole world.*

CONTENTS

INTRODUCTION

Welcome, Friends

Hello there, and welcome to *Growing Seasons*—a book I have dreamed about creating for a really long time. One of my biggest passions is to share stories that delight and encourage people—through my social media channels, through YouTube videos, through recipes and creative ideas—and so I've collected many of my favorite recipes, tips, DIYs, and personal stories in these pages. My hope is that this book will make you smile. I also hope it will inspire you to focus on what's most important in your life and encourage you to consciously choose to celebrate each and every day, no matter what season you happen to be in right now.

For those of you who don't know me yet, welcome, and I'm glad you're with me on this journey! Here's a very brief bio: my name is Kristin, and I am a content creator, entrepreneur, wife, and mom who currently lives in the Nashville area with my sweet family. While I am originally from Louisiana, I went to school in Florida before getting married to my husband, Marcus, and moving to LA, where I launched my business, Kristin Made. In 2021, we relocated to Tennessee to be closer to family and friends, and that same year, we welcomed our son, James, into the world. When I'm not busy with Kristin Made projects (or chasing James around!), you're most likely to find me baking in the kitchen, propagating houseplants, or off in the woods somewhere with my "boys" and our golden retrievers.

I suppose if you were to glance casually at my Instagram profile or the videos I post to YouTube, you could easily infer an entirely carefree life of ease. But while it's true that I do put a big emphasis on hope, fun, joy, and positivity in the content I create, that's not the whole story. For me, as for everybody, there have been plenty of hard times to go with the good ones, and I think it's important that we share our vulnerable, painful stories alongside the happy ones. The truth is, the past few years have been especially difficult. I've traveled some hard roads, and I have the scars and titanium pins to prove it. I've been challenged in ways that I never could have imagined, but as I've gone through seasons of sadness, fear, pain, and deep questioning, I've been shaped into the person I am today. I guess here is where I should stop and explain a bit. . . .

In early 2020, while the COVID-19 pandemic was sweeping the world and causing so much fear, pain, loss, and grief for people everywhere, I experienced an unrelated but deeply traumatic event—an experience that would dramatically affect my life and that would, ultimately, inspire the writing of this book.

On May 11, 2020—I'll never forget the date, because it's my sister's birthday—while riding bicycles in our quiet LA neighborhood, Marcus and I were the victims of a violent hit-and-run. In an attempt to escape police pursuit, the driver of a stolen car (a thief on the run) intentionally sped up and swerved toward us, crashing into both of us from behind. The impact threw us forward thirty feet. I landed on the sidewalk and just lay there for what felt like a long time. Nothing seemed real to me in those first moments. I could not understand where we were, what had happened, exactly, or why I was lying on the ground. Not far away, I could see that our bicycles were crushed. I was dizzy and disoriented, and I didn't know where Marcus was. Finally, I saw him lying nearby, unconscious and unmoving, in some stranger's front yard. But I couldn't go to him. I could barely sit up. Before long, I realized that my leg was broken. The pain was indescribable. Not being able to stand up—or move, really—was so scary. But the fear when I saw Marcus lying there in the grass was the worst part of all. When the ambulance arrived, the first thing the EMTs told us was that our helmets had saved our lives.

Marcus and I spent the next four weeks in the hospital. He had three surgeries, and I had six. Because of COVID, we had to be separated from each other for most of that period, and only one family member at a time could stay with us in the hospital—but not in our rooms. It was the longest thirty days of my life. I was in so much pain. I was scared and lonely, and every day, it seemed like the doctors needed new tests or scans or blood work done, so I was continually being carted through the hospital to be tended to by a new doctor or nurse at all hours of the day and night.

As a committed homebody and lifelong introvert, being in the hospital was a nightmare for me. Although I will forever be grateful for the incredible care I received during those weeks, I can honestly say that I've never felt so sad, so depressed, or so alone. The pain made it hard to sleep. I didn't want to eat, and I couldn't see Marcus. Most of the time, I didn't even have the energy to cry. And there were so many questions swirling in my head and troubling my heart. *Why in the world did this happen to us? What will this mean for Marcus's and my marriage? Am I ever going to be able to walk again? Will my injuries keep me from having babies?* For nearly twenty-four hours a day, as I lay awake and alone in the cold, sterile bubble of my isolated hospital room, attached to machines but detached from everyone in the world who could help me feel safe, a storm of fear and uncertainty raged inside me as my body tried to heal.

In time, though, I did begin to heal. The surgeries had been successful. Eventually, my appetite came back. Then, in late June, I was finally able to go home. Both our moms moved in with us and did everything for us (we are still so grateful for this loving help). Marcus's dad came in from Florida and built us wheelchair ramps so that we could go outside for fresh air and sunshine. After spending a few weeks in a wheelchair, I graduated to a grandma-style walker, and finally, I learned to get around with a cane.

Everything was hard: brushing my teeth, getting dressed, taking a bath—even getting a glass of water was a sweat-inducing chore. Still, with the help of my physical therapists, my strength returned. Slowly but surely, I began to walk on my own. Even after that, it was clear to me that my life would never be the same. There were steel pins in my hips and legs, and scars down the length of my leg that will never not be there. There were nightmares about the accident and a whole catalog of related fears and emotions that I am still learning to unpack and manage.

But while we spent months recuperating at home and learning to walk again, something beautiful and unexpected began to happen. I found myself with a newfound appreciation for . . . well, everything. All of a sudden, I felt a great surge of gratitude springing up inside of me for the simplest things: for fresh-baked bread, for long snuggles with my dogs, for my mom's treasured recipes, and for long, rambling, life-giving conversations with my sister and my friends. After so many days under the shadow of fear and pain and uncertainty, it was as if I was rediscovering the joy of life itself. Despite everything that happened, joy had endured. Marcus and I had so much to be thankful for. We had our lives. We had our home, friends, and family. We had each other.

The idea for *Growing Seasons* was born during those long months of recovery, while my body slowly healed and life steadily became "normal" again. It was then that I began to think about how to translate my newfound joy into something that could be an encouragement to others. For a long time, I had dreamed of putting together a book full of favorite recipes, ideas for interiors, and reflections on faith, family, and love. But it wasn't until after our accident, having weathered a surreal season of pain, fear, uncertainty, and, ultimately, joy, that I felt I had a real vision for what I wanted to say and why. I've come to believe that each season of life has its own purpose, its own valuable lessons to teach us. And that, simply put, is the heart and soul of this book.

With *Growing Seasons*, I want to inspire and encourage you to step into each day with courage and to embrace each season of life—whether it's a time of warmth and abundance or a time of wintry blues—with hope and joy. Just as each season of the calendar year has its own specific character, so, too, does each season of life have its own unique challenges and opportunities. Over the course of my extraordinarily difficult year, I learned that there is beauty to be found in each day and wonder to be experienced in every season.

Arranged according to the calendar year, from January to December, this book's twelve chapters feature ideas and insights that I hope will help you grow in your joy, creativity, outlook, and hope. Because the book follows the cycle of the calendar, you can jump in anywhere you like. You can start on page 1 and read straight through or dive into June or July if you're in a summery mood. It's totally up to you. Each chapter includes a personal story from me, a few of my favorite recipes, and a DIY or hosting-related activity that I hope will kick-start your creativity in one way or another. At the end of each chapter, I have added a single "reflection question" that I hope will help you think about areas of growth in your own life. All in all, I hope these pages are nourishing to you, wherever you are in your journey.

As I get older (and, I hope, wiser!), I am increasingly thankful for each and every season of life that I experience—both the bright, warm summers and the long, gray winters; the seasons of change and challenge; the moments of hardship and heartache. As long as we reach for the light, I believe we will continue to grow. We may not see ourselves changing. We may not feel it happening. And it may be painful at times. But as long as we have life, then we can have hope. As long as there is hope, there is room to grow.

kristin johns

A SEASON
OF BEGINNINGS

A NEW YEAR IS ALWAYS EXCITING, ISN'T IT? With the holiday season behind us and the warmer days of spring on the near horizon, a new year feels so full of potential. It's a fresh start—a time to begin again and make positive changes in the hope of ending the year as better versions of ourselves.

That said, New Year's resolutions have always overwhelmed me. In my whole life, I think I've only ever committed to two actual New Year's resolutions, both of which I abandoned and totally forgot about by Valentine's Day. Surprise, surprise, right?

I am someone who has to be careful when setting goals because I am both easily disappointed and easily discouraged by failure. Maybe you can relate. This means that spontaneous goals, or goals that force me into rigid patterns, or goals that are pressed upon me from external forces, don't really work; they aren't emotionally or practically feasible. What I've learned does work is setting goals that feel both attainable and worthwhile.

This book celebrates the fact that our lives are made up of "growing seasons"—times that mold us and stretch us, sometimes in joyful ways and sometimes in challenging ways—and the beginning of the year is a great time to pause and consider what kinds of growth we want to experience in the upcoming year. What goals are we setting? What seeds are we planting that will help set us on a path to becoming the person we want to be?

A simple way to choose a worthwhile goal starts with learning to ask the right kinds of questions. I do this by carefully considering any new opportunity alongside what I know about myself: my personality, my past experiences, my strengths and weaknesses. I've found that if I can answer the four questions below before stepping into almost any new endeavor, then there's a decent chance I'll be able to stick with it.

- What specifically do I want to achieve?

- What will it really take to get there?

- Why do I want to grow or change in this way?

- What is the positive good that will result in this kind of growth or change?

Answering these questions helps me explain to others—and to myself—why something is important enough to invest time, energy, and emotions in. These answers also assist me in sticking with my goals and remind me why I'm doing what I'm doing when things get hard or complicated. It's all about setting clear expectations. Without this clarity of purpose to sustain me when the going gets tough, I can easily lose interest, inspiration, and momentum and start spiraling into disappointment and discouragement. And then it's right back into bed and under the covers for me—where I can hide from my own failures and lack of discipline for a month or ten. Obviously, this is not a pattern of healthy growth. This is not the kind of friend, wife, or mother I want to be. I want to be someone who looks to the future with hope and confidence and who can work toward my goals in healthy ways—if possible, in ways that inspire others to chase their own goals and dreams.

Knowing that James will be watching everything that Marcus and I say and do as he grows up is absolutely the most humbling part of being a parent. We are the lens through which he will gain his understanding of the world and of himself. Already, he is watching us as we make plans, work toward our goals, struggle, fail, and decide whether or not to persevere. We believe that one of the best things we can give our son is a healthy perspective on what it means to look into the future. We want him to dream big, to learn the value of hard work, and to be resilient in pursuit of his goals, even if that means false starts, growing pains, and facing defeat along the way. And, as part of that journey, we want our son to truly know himself, to listen to his own instincts and intuition, to always consider the effect his choices have on others, to develop his own distinctive voice, and to be the kind of person who will work hard at things truly worth working hard for.

The more I think about these things, the more I realize that what I want for my son is also what I want for myself: to be someone who is always looking hopefully toward the future. To be someone with the ability to take the bad with the good and not give up; someone who is resilient in the face of adversity; someone who can forgive herself, not if but when she fails. By now, I know that this is not the work of a single season or a single year: it is the project of a lifetime.

So here's my goal for this year and for every year to come: continue to grow, one day at a time, month after month, season after season. Progress may be slow; change might be incremental. I will struggle, and I will certainly fail along the way, but I will press on. I guess this is now my "every year's resolution": keep listening, keep learning, be patient with myself and others along the way, and keep reaching for the light no matter how dark the season.

This is how I want to grow.

MY FAVORITE GREEN SMOOTHIE

Delicious, refreshing, and full of antioxidants, this green beauty is my go-to for a quick, healthy breakfast or post-workout pick-me-up.

For me, the best thing about smoothies is how easy it is to pack them full of greens without sacrificing that tasty "this is almost a milkshake" experience. Honestly, you can put as much spinach as you want in this simple smoothie, but thanks to the sweet frozen fruit, tangy ginger, and creamy milk, it's those rich and delicious flavors you're going to taste, not the greens. I love to switch up my smoothie recipes, but this is one I always go back to because it is such a perfect way to start the day—healthy greens and a burst of protein that provide long-lasting energy.

PREP TIME: 5 MINUTES

TOTAL TIME: 5 MINUTES

SERVES 2

2 handfuls of fresh baby spinach

1 frozen banana

1 cup coconut water

1 cup frozen pineapple chunks

½ teaspoon ground ginger

1 tablespoon chia seeds, plus more for garnish

1 scoop vegan vanilla protein powder*

Unsweetened vanilla almond milk to taste

Unsweetened shredded coconut for garnish

In a blender, combine the spinach, banana, coconut water, pineapple, ginger, chia seeds, protein powder, and almond milk, and blend until smooth. You can add more or less coconut water and milk depending on your desired thickness.

Garnish with chia seeds and unsweetened shredded coconut.

Note: If you're not a fan of almond milk, feel free to substitute your favorite plant-based milk alternative. Or if you want to skip the milk element altogether, that's also okay.

If you don't have protein powder on hand, no worries: this smoothie will still help you pack a ton of nutrients into your day.

A FRESH START

Five Ways to
Reimagine Any Room

The beginning of the new year is a great time to refresh your home! Simplicity is key, and here are five easy everyday tricks that I use to minimize clutter and maximize coziness while maintaining a sense of lightness. Using these as a guide, I'm able to keep our house feeling both tidy and welcoming even when I'm extra busy.

BRING THE OUTSIDE IN

Plants add a fresh, natural touch to any room. With their beauty and elegance, they're like organic art. Houseplants add so much life (literally) to our homes. From the dramatic fiddle-leaf fig to the tiniest cactus, they are living, breathing things that clean our air, provide fresh fragrances, and help make spaces feel calm and welcoming. Here are a few of the easiest plants to start with (in other words, these are some of the hardest houseplants to kill).

- **Monstera**: Adaptable to almost all light conditions and somewhat drought-tolerant, the monstera is a low-maintenance, stunning tropical plant.

- **Sansevieria**: This hardy plant will do just fine in any spot in the home, from low-light areas to places that get bright full sun. Sansevieria don't need a lot of water, are not sensitive to temperature changes, and don't require any special care.

- **Heartleaf philodendron:** This adaptable plant thrives in indirect light and actually suffers if exposed to bright sunlight. It likes to be consistently watered but is very forgiving if you forget to water it once in a while.

- **Hedgehog aloe:** A cousin of aloe vera, the hedgehog aloe plant needs a sunny spot in your home and can even be kept outside during the summer. This low-maintenance plant requires very little water, making it easy to care for.

FOCUS ON NATURAL MATERIALS

Tasteful and timeless, the materials, colors, and textures that come from nature never go out of style. And like decorating with plants, using these materials is a great way to bring the outside in.

There are three natural materials I incorporate into my home: rattan, leather, and wood. These are my favorite materials because they share a relatively neutral color palette, which means they complement one another no matter how they are used.

In addition to those "big three," I also love using dried pampas grass, vintage brass and copper items, terra-cotta pots, and ceramic jars as accent pieces. Playing with natural materials and a variety of textures is a perfect way to create a friendly, earthy atmosphere and add depth to your space while still keeping it calm and cohesive.

Bonus tip: I find a lot of these kinds of home goods at bargain prices in vintage and thrift shops, where they often have a gently used patina that adds another layer to their beauty.

KEEP THINGS FLEXIBLE

The more flexible you are with the design and layout of your rooms, the more variety you will be able to create in your home.

Incorporating artwork, photos, and frames is one of the most difficult parts of designing an interior. I love having artwork around my house, but I also enjoy moving things around and swapping out the art in my frames pretty often. So I've learned that the best way to keep things fresh is to keep things flexible.

I tend to get tired of big, bold artworks, gravitating instead toward subtle earth tones and geometric pictures and paintings. In addition, I've found that simple neutral picture frames are timeless and can be used in a variety of ways for many years. And instead of hanging your art on the wall, where it can feel "permanent," try placing framed photos and canvases on shelves, on windowsills, behind furniture, or even on the floor. This way, they can easily be moved, rearranged, or reimagined as the light—or your vibe—changes. The more flexible you are with your decorations and artwork, the more you can move things around, experiment, and keep things fresh.

COMMIT TO CLUTTER-FREE COUNTERTOPS

Nothing can kill the cozy vibe of a home like clutter, so fight to keep it out of sight!

In my experience, crowded and disorganized countertops are the biggest offenders. My rule of thumb is this: I only keep items out on my counter that I use often (more than two to three times per week) and that look beautiful in their own right. I love my KitchenAid stand mixer and use it several times a week, so it's allowed to live on my countertop. I use my blender often, but I wouldn't really say it's nice to look at, so it stays stowed in an easily accessible drawer.

It's amazing what a quick two-minute tidy-up can do for your space and for your mental health. Sometimes just taking a look at my kitchen counters and thinking *What can I store in the cabinets?* can make such a difference. Fighting countertop clutter is an ongoing battle, but I won't give up, and I'll never give in. You, too, can fight the good fight!

CUSTOMIZE STORAGE

It's amazing how this simple trick has made my domestic duties so much more enjoyable. Here's what I do: I buy all my everyday essentials (spices, nuts, flour, rice, cleaning supplies, and so on) in bulk, then transfer those items into more visually pleasing and/or reusable containers, refilling as needed. This strategy does three good things for us: (1) it's usually more cost-effective to shop this way, (2) it's a buying pattern that results in less waste and fewer trips to the store, and (3) it helps me create a calm and consistent home aesthetic. Many of these kinds of storage solutions can be found at thrift stores, garage sales, and flea markets. Since I started this practice, I have been amazed how happy these little changes have made me.

Some ways to try it out in your home:

- Wooden, wicker, and rattan baskets are perfect for hiding away pillows, blankets, and dog toys.

- Glass jars with either wooden or airtight lids are great for baking essentials.

- Small vintage apothecary-style jars are good for spices and small knickknacks.

- You can even find some nice logoless recycled plastic spray bottles for kitchen and bathroom cleansers.

REFLECTION

In what ways do you hope to grow during the year ahead, whether personally, professionally, emotionally, or spiritually? Try writing one of your goals down and placing it somewhere you will see it every day as a gentle reminder.

GETTING STARTED
WITH A SOURDOUGH STARTER

*There's nothing more comforting, relaxing, or satisfying than baking
your own bread. Best of all, homemade bread is an act of love that you
can share with those you treasure the most. But beware: once you begin
nurturing your own doughy starters, the art of parenting your little
loaves can become an obsession.*

Why is sourdough so special, you ask? Well, because of the fermentation process it undergoes, sourdough is easier to digest than many other breads. Also, sourdough is rich in lactic acid, which helps our bodies digest the bread's nutrients.

As anyone who's ever walked this road before will tell you, it can be intimidating to begin your sourdough journey. Why all this fear surrounding the ancient art of making bread? Because in order to make great sourdough, you have to first make a great sourdough starter, which will act as the leavening agent that brings the bread to life. The starter is what gives your loaf its unique taste and structure.

I adapted the King Arthur Baking guidelines, but I have found a few tips and tricks that make the process enjoyable and stress-free. Any bread lover can do this at home. Sure, it takes some time and careful attention, but what meaningful endeavor doesn't? Fear not, future bread baker: you can do this.

Now, then, let's stop talking and get started with our starter.

50 grams unbleached all-purpose flour, plus more for feeding your starter

50 grams whole wheat flour

100 grams room temperature water, plus more for feeding your starter

WHAT YOU'LL NEED

A clean nonreactive container, such as a glass bowl, with at least a one-quart capacity

A wooden spoon

A large piece of cheesecloth or tea towel

A large rubber band

An instant-read thermometer

A kitchen scale for weighing the ingredients

HOW I MAKE A NEW SOURDOUGH STARTER

Day 1: Let's go! Combine the flours and the cool water in a nonreactive container. Mix thoroughly with a wooden spoon until there's no dry flour left. Cover with a clean, dry piece of cheesecloth or a tea towel and secure the cover to the bowl with a rubber band. Allow to rest for 24 hours.

Day 2: At first, there might not be much visible change in your starter—just a little expansion or a few bubbles. But if you've followed the instructions above, something is definitely happening with your little baby. Either way, it's time to divide your starter for the first time and discard half of it. You can either trash this half or share it with a friend who wants to embark on her own sourdough adventure. After dividing, add about 1 cup fresh unbleached all-purpose flour and ½ cup cool water. Mix well, cover, and let the mixture rest at room temperature for another 24 hours.

Day 3: By now, you should be able to visibly see your starter bubbling and expanding. Hooray! This means it's happening— you're the proud parent of a growing sourdough starter. Now it's time to start "feeding" your starter twice a day. At each feeding, divide and discard half your starter, and add 1 cup fresh unbleached all-purpose flour and ½ cup cool water. Mix completely and let rest for about 12 hours, then repeat.

Day 4: Remember to feed your starter every 12 hours, dividing and discarding half each time.

Day 5: By this time, your little dough baby should have grown . . . a lot. Usually it will have doubled in volume, and there will be plenty of bubbles. There should also be a mild yeasty, bready aroma coming from the starter. If the starter hasn't risen much, or if there aren't many bubbles, then that means the starter isn't ready yet. In this case, continue to feed

→

every 12 hours for two more days, or until the starter is big and bubbly. Once the starter is ready, feed it one more time as usual. Since you've already done so much hard work, this is another great moment to give the discarded portion to a friend rather than trash it. There are also plenty of great ways to use your sourdough discard; I love to make sourdough pancakes or even chips with mine! Let your busy, bubbly starter rest at room temperature for 6 to 8 more hours. Be patient: you're almost ready to start baking.

Day 6: You're finally ready to use your sourdough starter to make bread. It's also time to establish a permanent home for your starter, a place where it can live and grow happily and contribute to the creation of countless future loaves and treats.

First, remove whatever quantity of starter you need for the recipe you want to make (typically no more than about 1 cup). If your recipe calls for more than 1 cup of starter, go ahead and give your starter a couple of extra feedings without discarding any: this way you'll have enough for your recipe and enough for the starter to stay active and thriving for your next baking adventure.

Move what's left of your starter into a sealed food-safe container. If you use a screw-top container, don't close it too tightly, because the starter needs to breathe. I call this remaining starter my reserve, and I will continue to feed it for months, using it for breads, sweet treats, and pizza dough (see page 151). Your reserve starter can be stored at room temperature or in the fridge.

But you should know this: if you store your reserve in the fridge, it only needs to be fed once a week (I set a reminder on my phone). If you store your reserve at room temperature, it will need to be fed daily, at around the same time each day . . . which is a lot of work. But if you want to use your starter to make fresh bread every day (yum! good for you!), then storing it at room temperature is best. I've done some experimenting over the years, and I've tried storing my reserve both ways. One thing I've found is that starter stored at room temperature tends to have a milder taste than starter kept in the fridge and fed once a week.

Now, this process is going to look a bit different depending on where you live in the world (altitude, temperature, humidity, and indoor climate can all have an impact on starter), so don't get discouraged along the way. Follow the steps above, ask a friend in your area for tips, look around on YouTube for troubleshooting guides, and please let me know how it goes—how it grows—for you. Good luck, bakers!

A FEW TIPS

(FROM SOMEONE WHO LEARNED THE HARD WAY)

I usually mix equal amounts of all-purpose flour and whole wheat flour. You can also use all one type of flour or try different types of flours, which will result in different flavors.

The most important thing to keep in mind when measuring is that the amount of flour and water should be exactly equal.

Your water should be between 80°F and 90°F. This is crucial.

Your starter will be most successful if your kitchen is a warmish room (between 65°F and 72°F).

Stay away from bleached flours, because they don't contain the wild yeast needed during the fermentation process.

Signs that your starter is ready: it's doubled in size, has a tangy smell, and floats on the surface of water, usually between five to ten days!

Since you have to discard a portion of "living" starter each day in the beginning to make room for proper growth, consider placing your discarded portions in mason jars and gifting them to friends.

A SEASON
OF INTIMACY

ONCE UPON A TIME, BACK WHEN MARCUS and I were still dating long distance but not yet engaged (I was living in Florida, and he was living in LA), he invited me to come out to California for Valentine's Day. Of course, I was excited to have any excuse to visit him, and I thought it was really thoughtful of him to arrange a trip around this sweet little holiday. On the flight to LA, I started to wonder what he had up his sleeve for the day itself. We hadn't talked about it ahead of time, but I could sense he was planning something special. If you know anything about Marcus, you probably know that (1) he's really good at a lot of things (writing, acting, singing, songwriting, comedy, building things, and on and on), and (2) whenever he decides to go big on a project, he goes *big*. The wheels of my romantic imagination started spinning: What was he up to? A sunset horseback ride on the beach? A picnic in Malibu? Something involving a train or a sailboat or a fancy restaurant? I had no idea! But what I was sure of was this: Marcus was going to make this Valentine's Day over the top and unforgettable.

But I was wrong. Okay, I was half wrong. Marcus definitely did make that Valentine's Day unforgettable, but not in the way I had expected. Not in a bold, flashy, "look how thoughtful and romantic I am" sort of way. It wasn't over the top at all. Instead, he did something simple, something I wouldn't have guessed he would do in a thousand years. Something that was specifically for me. That night, he made me dinner at home. Fresh salad and pasta in a yummy sauce, a bottle of red wine, and my favorite chocolate cake from Trader Joe's. Now, this might not seem like a big deal to you, but for anyone who knows Marcus, making this meal was, in fact, a very big deal.

Marcus is good at a lot of things, but cooking is not one of them. In fact, during the first year that we dated, I never saw him prepare a single meal more complicated than a bowl of cereal or a smoothie (and the smoothie was an event, let me tell you). So when he surprised me with a home-cooked meal that he had planned, shopped for, prepped, cooked, and cleaned up before I got there, I was blown away. A cozy night at home with good food is one of my favorite things in the world, and because Marcus knew that about me, his gift was to create a special evening that he knew would surprise me and that I would love. He knew I didn't want to spend Valentine's Day on a horse ride on the beach or in a Ferris wheel or with a celebrity chef. I'm sure I would have enjoyed all those things (who wouldn't?), but none of those grand gestures would have been as intimate as the meal he prepared at home for me. It was his way of saying, "Even though cooking isn't really my thing, I see you, I love you, and I want you to know that I am willing to grow for the sake of this relationship."

When I think of intimacy, I picture a kind of easy closeness between people. A peacefulness that is hard to describe but that you can feel. For me, intimacy is different from love—though I think it comes from love—because intimacy is such a deep experience, one in which I can be fully myself right where I am. I can be still and relaxed in the present because I know that this relationship stretches back into the past and will continue to grow into the future.

We often think of intimacy only in the context of romantic relationships, but it's part of all our important relationships. At the moment, I feel really lucky to have so many close relationships in my life: those with Marcus, James, my mom and dad, my sister and sister-in-law, my nieces and nephews, and my best friends. Each of these relationships has its own unique history of memories and shared experiences and inside jokes. And even though most of these people don't live near to me, and we

can't always be physically close, it's this depth of love and memories that makes each relationship so rich—so that when we do get together in person, it's like no time has passed at all and we can just pick up the relationship right where we left off.

But this level of intimacy needs to be nurtured. I doubt that I will ever stop being close with my sister or my college roommates or my husband, but nonetheless, all these relationships require care and affection in order for a healthy closeness to sustain itself. Even if it's just a wink and a smile at Marcus in the midst of a busy day at home or a text message sent around the world to my best friend in Uganda or making space for an intentional "tell me how you're really doing" conversation over coffee, intimacy requires work. But it's the work of love. And in my experience, I've found that the fruit of intentional time spent with the people I love is always a deeper level of friendship. And that's a gift we get to share with each other.

The older I get, the more precious authenticity and intimacy have become in my life. In a culture that seems to be endlessly chasing trends, likes, followers, subscribers, and ever-larger audiences made up of strangers . . . I think what I truly want more than anything else, and what I want for others, is to experience the beauty and joy of deep friendships rooted in love.

SIMPLE, SCRUMPTIOUS BANANAS FOSTER

*If you're looking for a good Valentine's Day or date-night treat,
this super-easy recipe for Bananas Foster is both delicious and incredibly
simple. It's a favorite around our house and never disappoints.*

One Valentine's Day a few years ago, I surprised Marcus with this simple, yummy version of Bananas Foster, and ever since, it's been a favorite sweet treat around our house. This recipe has all the "ooh" and flavor without the challenge of lighting anything on fire. This method was handed down from my dad, who used to make this for us all the time when we were little.

PREP TIME: 5 MINUTES

COOK TIME: 5 MINUTES

TOTAL TIME: 10 MINUTES

SERVES 2 TO 4

2 tablespoons unsalted butter

4 firm, ripe bananas, cut into 1-inch slices

½ cup firmly packed brown sugar

1 teaspoon vanilla extract

½ teaspoon ground cinnamon

Pinch of table salt

Vanilla ice cream for serving

Melt the butter in a medium saucepan over medium heat. Add the bananas and stir until softened, about 2 minutes.

Stir in the brown sugar, vanilla, cinnamon, and salt.

Reduce the heat to low and stir constantly, for about 2 more minutes, or until the bananas are caramelized and the sauce thickens.

Pour the bananas and the sauce into a cute bowl, and top with a scoop of vanilla ice cream.

Grab two spoons and share with someone you love.

GATHER IN CLOSE

Curating Space(s)

for Connection

Two common inhibitors that make intimacy tough for any relationship are distance and distraction. For example, sometimes I feel super close with my sister, who lives far away, while I feel distant from a good friend who lives nearby. At other times, I will be sitting on the sofa right next to Marcus or my mom or James, and my focus is a million miles away. So intimacy is never determined by just one thing, especially because it involves two or more people. In other words, intimacy is complicated. It can be hard. It often takes work.

But since the goal of intimacy is closeness, there are some things we can do in our physical space to help nurture connectedness. I've outlined four simple ways that your body, your furniture, and the rooms of your home can encourage greater intimacy with the people in your life.

PUT THE PHONE AWAY & ENJOY INTENTIONAL TIME

Okay, putting the phone away is obvious, but it's also hard, especially because our phones have become essential to so much of our daily lives. But if I want to spend true quality time with anyone in my life, I have to put my phone away. It's nonnegotiable. Try it during your next gathering and see what happens when you're with your spouse, your kids, or your friends. You might be shocked at the difference you feel.

COZY UP CLOSE

Physical closeness can really help facilitate emotional intimacy and great conversations. I think this is why I love dark-stained wooden pub

booths, window seats, and all other manner of private seating nooks. These are the best places to sit close and share secrets (and cake!). Now, don't get me wrong, I love a roomy, overstuffed couch, but when it comes to having a serious talk or an overdue heart-to-heart, small spaces are better.

If you want to have a deep convo, choose the love seat instead of the giant sofa. Choose the little round café table instead of a seat at the bar, and whatever you do, choose a space where loud music and sports on TV won't steal your attention. Going on a drive can accomplish the same thing: even though you can't always see eye to eye while driving, being seated together within such a small space can provide opportunities for great conversation and closeness. Whenever we "bring it in close," it's just easier to hear the other person, see eye to eye, and reach out and make a physical connection. If it helps to have a soft, shareable blanket nearby, make it happen. Coziness and connectedness often go hand in hand.

DIVIDE & CONQUER YOUR SPACE

Sometimes a large physical space needs to be subdivided into smaller spaces that are more conducive to intimacy. If you watch kids at play, you'll notice that they do this very naturally all the time. They play under the kitchen table or under the stairs; they build "forts" with blankets and quilts; they love little tents and tipis and hidey-holes where the imagination can run wild. Small spaces are private, cozy, and free from outside distractions; they are more intimate.

So if you have extra-tall ceilings or big, wide-open rooms in your home or office, you might try moving things around and creating smaller "rooms within a room." There are countless ways to divide and conquer a big space to make it inviting for intimacy. For example, arrange several small seating areas, or consider placing a pair of tall-back chairs facing each other near a window with a view. You can also use plants or a sculpture or a Japanese-style screen to define a space. Or how about placing a pair of soft beanbag-style chairs in a corner by the fireplace? Or arranging an extra-plush rug and a pair of oversize pillows on the floor? Changes like this really invite people to make themselves comfortable. And when people are comfortable, they open up and chat.

Whatever you do, try to stay open-minded and flexible. Move things around and experiment with your family or when guests come over. It might take a few attempts, but through trial and error, you'll figure out what works and what doesn't. Watch to see which spaces people naturally gravitate toward. If people are gathering, then it's working.

SHARE STORIES

Stories are one of the best ways to connect with others through shared experiences. Here are just a few ideas for using your home as a place where people gather to share stories.

- Create a curated lending library where you actively offer to let guests borrow your favorite books. Then, when they're done reading, invite them back over to return the book, discuss it, share a meal or pot of tea, and pick out their next read. This way, your books can bring people together and inspire all kinds of intimate conversations about life, art, travel, family, and/or hobbies.

- Host an evening of cozy "fireside chats" around a backyard bonfire, patio firepit, or just around the fireplace. Ask guests to bring a good story to tell. What kinds of stories, you ask? Funny? Inspiring? Spooky? Sure, why not?! Okay, it's a little old-fashioned, but it could be amazing to see what kinds of stories come out of a gathering like this. Whatever happens, it will be memorable, which always helps nurture intimacy.

- Create a regular listen-and-learn session with a friend or partner. Here's how it works: you and a friend meet up, sit close together, and take turns sharing information about something you've been learning recently. You can talk about pop culture, science, history, nature—anything. And each session should definitely include snacks and drinks! This can be as serious or silly as you want it to

be and can last as long as you like, though I recommend a time limit of ten minutes per "presentation." There aren't any other rules, but it's a way to share something you're interested in with someone else in an intentional way. To add an element of fun and mystery, don't tell each other ahead of time what you're going to discuss.

REFLECTION

Is there a person in your life with whom you wish you could be closer—maybe your mom or a sibling, a friend or a romantic partner? What are a few ways that you could invest in that relationship to help the intimacy grow?

THE PERFECT
CHARCUTERIE BOARD
AT HOME

We love game nights at our house. It's a great way to go gadget-free for a few hours and focus on the best things in life: friends, fun, and obviously, food! When I host a game night, I want the focus to be on spending time with my friends, not being stuck in the kitchen cooking, so I build a creative charcuterie board that can serve as an all-night snack station for hungry guests.

———————————

Charcuterie is a French term for prepared meat products such as ham, salami, and prosciutto, but there is much more to the art of building a great charcuterie board than just piling up various meats. The trick is to bring together the right variety of complementary finger foods that can both stand on their own *and* go with everything else on offer. I also want the combined elements to please the unique palates of a group. Pita chips are great . . . but pita chips dipped in homemade hummus are even better. Add a side of organic Kalamata olives and spicy chorizo slices—this is the magic of charcuterie!

When I'm building a charcuterie board for my game nights, I take into account not just how the individual elements taste, but also how they look. Half the fun of any charcuterie board is crafting the presentation. A proper charcuterie board should elicit at least a few gasps of "Oh, wow" when guests wander through the kitchen.

Here are some basic guidelines I follow . . . but feel free to mix and match and get creative!

Mounding a few varieties of nuts, such as Marcona almonds and
pecans, between meats and cheeses adds a nice texture and crunch.
It also allows you to easily fill in any gaps in your board.

I love using fresh fruits such as grapes, pomegranates,
and strawberries, not only for their flavor, but also
for the beautiful pop of color they add to the board.

Focus on getting three to five good-quality cheeses and meats, then run wild from there.

MARCH

A SEASON
FOR NESTING

HOME IS MY HAPPY PLACE. THIS HAS BEEN true for pretty much my whole life: when I was a kid, my room was my perfect little sanctuary—always clean, organized exactly the way I wanted it, and off-limits to trespassers. These days, home isn't just where I eat and sleep and store my stuff, it's also where Marcus and I do nearly all our work. Plus, over the years, I've learned that my home is the place where I can be most creative, whether that's in the kitchen, making videos, or running my business. So this is why it's so important to me that my home be a calm and comfortable place.

When Marcus and I decided to relocate from LA to Tennessee, even though I knew it was the right move for our family and I was excited about it, I had to let go of a house I loved, a home full of amazing memories and experiences. Making this move, we knew there would be a period of transition as we shifted our lives cross-country. Our top priority was finding a temporary place where we could settle in before James was born. Then, we thought, we would spend a few months looking for a house that we could buy and move right into. Little did we know that this would be a nearly two-year process.

We packed 90 percent of our belong-ings into a shipping crate and didn't know how long it would be before we would see them again. Then, for about twenty months, we lived out of suitcases and moving boxes, hopping from place to place every few months while we searched for a permanent place to live.

Of course, I'm thankful that during that prolonged period, we always had a roof over our heads. But as you can imagine, for a certified homebody like me, that extra-long period of transition was pretty unsettling. The cozy sanctuary I had worked so hard to make back in California was long gone, and I didn't know when I would get to start making a home again. When James arrived, my desire for a space where I could nest was almost overwhelming. I thought about it all the time, constantly feeling anxious, impatient, and easily annoyed. Everyone said we would find what we were looking for eventually, and I knew that was true. But meanwhile, I was an emotional wreck. I just wanted to know where the heck we were going to live.

In the end, we did find a house that we loved, located on some wild acreage where James and his future siblings could run around and explore and where we hope to someday raise some animals. The house itself needed some renovations before we could move in, so that meant several more months spent in a temporary place. But this was a house—the house—that we felt was well worth the wait.

Looking back, I can see that most of my anxiety during that period of transition was rooted in fear and uncertainty about the future. There were hard parts to that process, but there were a lot of great things, too, especially in those early months after James was born. It was amazing to discover the beauty and culture of a new city and state with Marcus and to be closer to so many friends and family members we love. While we were house hunting, we got to meet a lot of new people and explore cute towns and neighborhoods. It was a time of feeling somewhat unsettled, yes, but it was also a time ripe with potential and possibility.

As I reflect back on the long waiting period, I wish I had allowed myself to be more present in the moment, more thankful, and more at peace with where we were during that strange season. My heart and mind are often looking off into the distance, even when there is beauty and purpose and opportunity right in front of me. I want to grow in this area. I want to be able to be content wherever I am, to soak up whatever moment or season I am in, no matter what the future might hold.

I know this is easier said than done. But one little life hack that has been helpful to me is a daily meditation that I whisper to myself whenever I feel anxiety creeping up on me. In moments like this, I say to myself, "Be here now; this is where you need to be." Essentially, this is what Jesus said during the Sermon on the Mount: "Therefore do not worry about tomorrow, for tomorrow will worry about itself. Each day has enough trouble of its own" (Matt. 6:34). This is both a huge challenge and a huge comfort for me. I'm learning that I need to actively focus on today—each and every day—so that I don't miss out on the lessons and blessings right in front of me, right now.

Wherever you are in your life, whether you're between jobs or between life stages or between relationships or between houses, I hope you can find some beauty and hope in the moment you are in, even if that moment is a transition. It's not easy, I know. It's a struggle for me most days. It often feels far easier to worry and obsess about what is going to happen next. But instead of fear and anxiety and distraction, today I want to choose patience and peace and hope in the future. I know that everything has a season and that nothing lasts forever. And sure, maybe the beauty and lessons are sometimes not so obvious. They can be hard and painful and confusing. But all this helps shape us, strengthen us, and grow us into the people we are meant to be.

MOM'S CAJUN CRAWFISH ÉTOUFFÉE

My mom is the queen of refining and tweaking southern recipes until they are absolutely perfect. Visit her house most days of the year, and she's likely to have something spicy simmering in a pot or something extra-special slow-cooking in the oven. At our house, southern food—specifically, the Cajun food she grew up with—was the epitome of comfort food. And it still is! To this day, the aroma of Mom's étouffée can warm my soul and make my mouth water. Whenever someone asks me, "What's your all-time favorite meal?" the answer is easy: my mom's Cajun crawfish étouffée.

As a kid growing up in Louisiana (and, later, Florida), I didn't really understand much about the rich food culture of the South. I just knew that the food tasted amazing. I was raised on crawfish boils, shrimp and grits, gumbo, jambalaya, po'boys, bread pudding, Key lime pie, and crawfish étouffée, of course. Now that I've learned a bit more about the fascinating blend of cuisines that came together to lay the foundation of southern cooking—French, Caribbean, Latin, Native American, and African, just to name a few—it makes this unique food culture even more special to me.

After some begging on my part, my mom agreed to share her legendary étouffée recipe with me—and, of course, I had to share it with you. There's never been a cold winter day that can't be improved by a big, warm bowl of this spicy crawfish étouffée.

PREP TIME: 20 MINUTES

COOK TIME: 30 MINUTES

TOTAL TIME: 50 MINUTES

SERVES 4

4 tablespoons butter

4 tablespoons all-purpose flour

1 medium yellow or white onion, chopped

4 cloves garlic, chopped

2 teaspoons Tony Chachere's Original Creole Seasoning or CeCe's Cajun Seasoning (opposite)

Salt and pepper to taste

1 pound fresh or thawed frozen parboiled Louisiana crawfish tail meat

2 cups chicken stock

Cooked white rice for serving

1 tablespoon chopped fresh parsley for garnish

Melt the butter in a large pan or pot over medium heat.

Add the flour and stir constantly with a wooden spoon for 5 minutes, or until the roux turns a light chocolate-brown color. Watch carefully so that the roux doesn't burn.

Add the onion and garlic. Cook, stirring frequently, for 5 minutes, until the vegetables are soft.

Stir in the Creole seasoning, salt, and pepper.

Gradually add the stock.

Reduce the heat and simmer, stirring occasionally, for 20 to 30 minutes.

Add the crawfish tails to the pot and allow to warm through.

Serve over white rice and garnish with fresh parsley.

CECE'S CAJUN SEASONING

1½ teaspoons smoked paprika

1½ teaspoons garlic powder

1½ teaspoons fine kosher salt

1½ teaspoons onion powder

1 teaspoon black pepper

½ teaspoon dried oregano

1 teaspoon cayenne pepper

½ teaspoon dried parsley

1 teaspoon white pepper

½ teaspoon dried thyme

1 teaspoon dried basil

1 dried bay leaf

Combine all ingredients and store in an airtight container.

TIPS

Want a deeper, richer flavor? Extend the simmering time before adding the crawfish. Mom says it's okay to let it simmer for a few hours, but you might need to add more stock along the way.

I often make a double batch, then freeze half and save it for a rainy or extra-busy day when I don't feel like cooking.

FRESH AND CLEAN

A Simpler,
More Satisfying Spring Clean

Anytime you feel like you need a deep and satisfying refresh that goes beyond your typical daily tidy-up, you can use these tips to fight clutter and reset any part of your home, no matter what time of year it is. So tie up your hair, open up some windows, and crank up your favorite playlist—it's time to deep clean!

START IN THE KITCHEN

This is often the biggest part of my spring cleaning project, but when you tackle the biggest task first, everything else feels achievable. My kitchen cleanup strategy is simple but effective.

1. **Pull most everything out of the drawers and cupboards.** If there are items that need to be washed, throw them in the dishwasher so they can get clean while you do the rest. If there is anything that belongs in another room, toss it all in a big basket or bag and deal with it later. Priorities, people! Right now I'm all about the deep clean and can't get distracted by filing gift cards or looking for lost key rings.

2. **Vacuum and wipe down the insides of the drawers and cupboards**. I often find I'm vacuuming up months' worth of crumbs and granola dust! Use a natural cleaning spray and washable cloths to scrub and wipe everything down. And when I say everything, I mean *everything*; every single surface you can reach.

3. **Take a quick inventory of what you own**. Before I put anything back, I do a serious assessment. Do I still need all these things in my kitchen? Are we ever going to eat these cans of kidney beans that have been collecting dust for nine months? Are these Tupperware containers without lids actually worth keeping? Why are there dog treats in the cutlery drawer? Why do I have seven bowls that belong to my sister-in-law? (I need to return those!) I think you get it. Once I've done my honest assessment, I only put back those things I am sure I want to keep and know we will use or eat. Anything else has to go to the recycling bin or donation box. Taking this inventory at least once a year will help you feel like you're not just accumulating stuff (and if you ever move, you will be so thankful!).

Once I'm done in the kitchen, I make myself a nice big latte, sit back, and enjoy the satisfaction of a deeply cleaned, perfectly purged kitchen. Of course, it will only stay this organized for about an hour, so better enjoy it while I can, right?

BREEZE THROUGH THE BATHROOM

Two common challenge areas in the bathroom are (1) disorganized shelves that need some love and (2) cluttered drawers where expired makeup, loose flossing tools, and all sorts of little knickknacks lurk. The steps are similar to what you did in the kitchen.

1. **Pull everything out and wipe down the insides of the drawers and cabinets.** Go ahead and put the shower curtain in the washer, then thoroughly clean and disinfect all the surfaces.

2. **Assess and prioritize what's worth keeping**. Then purge!

3. **Only put back those things you know you will use.** Later, when I reopen my drawers or bathroom cupboards, I get such a delightful surprise when I see that everything is in its proper place. Seriously— there is nothing like opening a perfectly organized skin-care drawer!

CONQUER YOUR CLOSETS

Every home is different, and most homes have a variety of storage and closet spaces, each with its own set of challenges. (In my experience, closets overflowing with sports gear are the worst!) At my house, there are three types of closets that always need a refresh come springtime: the coat closet, the linen closet, and my bedroom closet, where I keep my clothes.

1. **The coat closet:** Typically, I wait to do my biggest spring clean until we're pretty sure winter is gone for good so that I can also put away coats, gloves, and other cold-weather items at the same time. After you put away your winter gear, do a basic reorganization of the remaining items before adding lighter jackets and raincoats. I love this process because it makes me eager for all the spring and summer fun to come.

2. **The linen closet:** Towels and linens are kind of like socks: somehow we always have more than we need, and remarkably, none of them ever matches. Spring is a great time to go through all your linens. If anything has holes or megastains, I hand it over to Marcus for use in his workshop. Get rid of or repurpose your old towels and linens, take note of what you might need to replace, then organize and neatly fold the remaining items.

3. **The clothes closet**: Purging clothes is often the hardest and most time-consuming task, so I follow a basic rule of thumb: if I haven't worn an item for an entire year, it's time to donate it to someone who will love it more than I do. Here's an easy way to make this less of a chore.

   • Pull all your clothes out of your closet. Designate one bag or box for giveaways and one for trash.

   • Immediately put anything that has holes or megastains in the trash bag (or repurpose it for crafts or workroom projects).

- Among the remaining items, if there's anything you haven't worn for a year, or that no longer fits, put it in the giveaway bag.

- Do a quick sweep and wipe down the surfaces, then organize everything you're keeping and put it back in.

One way to make this fun is to do a swap with friends. Before I take my bag of purged clothing to a donation center, I will often ask my girlfriends if they want to look through it. They always do. And sometimes they bring over their own boxes of clothes, and we all find something new to us that we like and will wear. Whatever's left after this I donate to a local charity shop.

You did it! That wasn't so bad, was it? And now you have a fresh, clean, and tidy home to enjoy . . . at least for a few minutes—or until the dogs, the kids, and life itself start to undo all your hard work. Time for another coffee!

REFLECTION

Is there a difficult transition happening in your life right now? Or maybe there's a big change up ahead on the horizon. Reflecting on how that makes you feel, take a deep breath and remind yourself that you have faced changes and challenges before and that you are stronger because of the growing pains you felt along the way.

ROSEMARY FOCACCIA

*I first encountered fresh-baked rosemary focaccia while traveling
in Italy one summer. It's no exaggeration to say that I've never
been the same. This salty, simple, and highly versatile bread has
been around since Roman times for very good reason. Here's my
easy-to-make take on this Italian classic.*

Legend has it that focaccia originated in the Italian city of Genoa, where it is still prepared
with just a few ingredients and baked in a rectangular shape, as it is in this recipe. The day I
tasted fresh-baked Italian rosemary focaccia for the first time, when Marcus and I traveled to
Italy together in 2016, I knew I would never be the same. Focaccia was our go-to snack while
we were out and about in Cinque Terre. Most days, we ate it for breakfast and/or lunch. Then
we carried it in our day packs while hiking up the coast, and we devoured it after long after-
noons playing in the sea. This simple bread holds a special place in my memory and in my heart.
Just the smell of baking focaccia can transport me back to the sunny shores of Cinque Terre.

Back home, focaccia was one of the first breads I ever learned to make myself, and it's still
one of my favorites! What I love most about this recipe is that I can customize it depending
on the food I'm serving it with, the toppings I happen to have at hand, or whatever I'm craving on a given day. So once you master the basics, feel free to make this recipe your own: add
sun-dried tomatoes if you like or an olive garnish or mix in a handful of your favorite salty
cheese. It's like a taste of Italy—at home!

For best results, enjoy this bread fresh out of the oven while sitting with the sun on your face.

PREP TIME: 1 DAY PLUS
3 HOURS, INCLUDING TIME
FOR THE DOUGH TO RISE

BAKING TIME: 30 MINUTES

TOTAL TIME: 1 DAY, 3½ HOURS

SERVES 8

2½ cups warm water
(about 110°F)

2 cups room temperature
water

1 packet (7 grams or 2¼
teaspoons) active dry yeast

2 teaspoons honey

5 cups all-purpose flour

2½ teaspoons flaky sea
salt, plus more for topping
if desired

8 tablespoons olive oil,
divided

Leaves of 2 sprigs fresh
rosemary (optional)

Handful of cherry or grape
tomatoes, halved
(optional)

Minced garlic (optional)

In a medium bowl, whisk together the water, yeast, and honey and let sit for 5 minutes, or until the yeast is foamy.

In a large bowl, combine the flour and salt. Add the yeast mixture and bring the dough together with your hands or a spatula until a shaggy ball forms.

Coat a large mixing bowl with 3 tablespoons of the olive oil and place the dough inside. Drizzle with 1 tablespoon of the remaining olive oil and spread it around so that it coats the dough. Cover the bowl with plastic wrap or a damp tea towel and place it in the fridge. You want the dough to rise for at least 8 hours and up to 24 hours. The dough will double in size and look bubbly.

Take the dough out of the fridge and gently shape it into a neat ball by folding it over itself.

Coat a deep rectangular baking pan with 2 tablespoons of the olive oil and transfer the dough ball to the baking pan. Use your hands to stretch the dough into a rectangular shape. Don't worry about making it fit perfectly all the way to the corners of the pan. Cover the pan with a damp tea towel and let the dough rise in a warm area of your house for another 3 hours.

Preheat the oven to 375°F. Once the dough has risen, use your fingers to indent or dimple the dough. You want to press firmly but not poke through to the bottom of the pan. Drizzle the dough with the remaining 2 tablespoons of olive oil. Top with rosemary, tomatoes, garlic, and a few pinches of flaky sea salt if desired. Bake for 20 to 30 minutes, or until the dough is golden.

A SEASON
FOR PLANTING

APRIL IS THE TIME OF YEAR WHEN WE PLANT tiny seeds into the softening earth so that in the not-too-distant future we will be able to harvest good things—things that nourish and delight ourselves and others, things worth sharing and celebrating. It might sound a little cheesy, but I can't help but think of our dreams as seeds—seeds that require care and patience and love in order to grow.

Marcus and I have known so many people who have wild and wonderful ideas for ways to help people in a big way or who are passionately pursuing creative projects (sometimes for years!) until they become a tangible reality. I love these kinds of people: dreamers are the ones who move the world forward. They challenge and inspire us and encourage us to think and see in new ways. I've heard it said that we all have at least one great story to tell, and if I had to guess, I bet we all also have at least one meaningful dream that's worth pursuing in our lives.

I sometimes wish *I* had one specific big dream with the potential to change the world. But I don't naturally gravitate toward big dreams. I admire ambition, though my goals are usually pretty practical and relatively humble. I'm more of a doer than a dreamer. And I like for ideas and projects to grow slowly and organically so that I can learn as I go and try to keep my mind wrapped around what is happening along the way. For better or worse, I always prefer order over chaos and calm over conflict, which means that, even when I believe in something, I typically tiptoe into every new adventure. That was certainly the case when I set out to produce my first YouTube video, back in 2015.

As he does with so many of the adventures in my life, Marcus played a big part in helping me transform my idea into reality. Always a force for positive, forward motion, he encouraged me not to worry too much about the technical side of things but to just go for it. He told me, "It doesn't have to be perfect." That was easy for him to say: he'd been writing, recording, and editing videos for years. I had never tried it before, and now I was considering making a YouTube channel of my own.

I had a lot of questions. First of all, I didn't know how to light or film a video properly, and I certainly didn't know how to edit one. There were also all the emotional questions about the project: Why did I want to do this? Who (if anyone) would ever want to watch a video made by me? What did I have to say? Where did I think this would all lead? In other words, what was the point? But I didn't let my inexperience hold me back. From my little bedroom in my little college house, I recorded and edited my first "Ask Kristin" video, featuring a cameo from a cat and lighting from a crappy old desk lamp.

Before posting that first video—on April 16, 2015—I felt so many fears: the fear of looking stupid, the fear of failure, the fear of rejection, the fear that my friends and family would think the whole idea was weird. In fact, as I look back on it, my biggest fear of all wasn't about failure. It was about being judged by others. My mom was going to see this video—and my roommates and Marcus and Marcus's friends and maybe all my old high school classmates and old boyfriends and my grandma!

The truth is, I was scared. I nearly backed out about a hundred times. Even after the file was uploaded to my YouTube channel, it took me a *very long time* before I was ready to hit the Make Public button on that first video. I paced around the house for hours, second-guessing everything. It seems a little bit dramatic now, but I think I had the sense that there might be no going back once I published that video. Finally, I pulled the trigger and went through with it: I closed my eyes, held my breath, and hit Publish. And that single decision changed my whole life.

Almost right away, kind viewers told me that they loved what I had made and started asking when I would share another video. That little bit of encouragement and support was so huge for me and gave me the confidence that I had made the right choice—to push past the doubts and fears in my head. This support gave me the courage to keep going.

That first year, I went on to make twenty-one YouTube videos They were light, silly, and creative videos about things that I cared about back then, from makeup and hair tutorials to videos I made with my family (the "My Boyfriend Does My Makeup" and "How Well Does My Mom Know Me" videos still crack me up, by the way). During that time, I was just learning as I went along, hoping that each video would be a little bit more watchable and a bit funnier or more inspiring than the last. When I started, I had no idea that YouTube could be or would be such a big part of my life and career. Looking back, I'm so glad I didn't let my fear of judgment stop me from taking a chance.

I'm pretty sure that if I had let my fears hold me back, I would have missed out on many of the opportunities that, today, give me so much joy and purpose. If I hadn't taken a risk on that first YouTube video, who knows? Maybe I would never have had the chance to build and launch my business, Kristin Made. And I certainly would never have had the chance to connect with so many people around the world, from engaged followers on social media to the individuals I've met in person and the talented team I get to work with each and every day. Not to mention that I might not have had the chance to write the book you're holding in your hands right now.

If I'm being totally real, I should tell you that I still usually hesitate a few moments before publishing any new video to YouTube. The shadow of fear and uncertainty is still there. Maybe it always will be, and maybe that's okay. Maybe it's the conquering of our fears—both big and small—that ends up shaping the course of a day or a career or a lifetime. There's a lot to be afraid of in this life, no question about that. But there are also a lot of things to hope for and to work toward. I've come to believe that our dreams are the truest expression of what we believe about the world and our place in it. Whenever we dream about doing big things, it's likely because we believe that big things can be a force for good in the world and are, therefore, worth doing.

If there's a dream in your heart or an idea in your head that just won't go away, you should nurture that little seed of hope. Move as fast or as slow as you need to. Good things take time, you know. But I hope you will always be willing to move out of your comfort zone. Don't let fear guide you. Take that first step and see what happens. Confidence comes with experience, and experience comes by doing, sometimes over and over and over again. You might fail. In fact, you probably will. And that's okay. But you'll never know until you let hope inspire you to take action. After that, who knows what good things might grow from the seeds of your dreams?

SUNNY CITRUS KALE SALAD

Kale is tricky to figure out, but once you realize the easy secret to getting it nice and tasty, it's bound to become your new favorite green!

Kale is one of the healthiest things you can put into your body. Kale is loaded with antioxidants, vitamin C, vitamin K, minerals, and beta-carotene. Plus, once I learned how to properly prepare kale, I really came to love it and have started using it in lots of ways.

This salad is a great introduction to kale. The ingredients are simple and fresh, and you likely already have several of them at home. But the secret to making a great kale salad is the massaging of the leaves. I know it sounds silly, but take your time with it—it breaks down some of the leaves' toughness and will make all the difference in the world when you sit down to eat. The citrus from the lemon and orange juices works its magic to soften the kale even more and really brightens the overall flavor, making this the perfect salad for any sunny spring day.

PREP TIME: 10 MINUTES

TOTAL TIME: 10 MINUTES

SERVES 3 TO 4

FOR THE DRESSING

¼ cup extra-virgin olive oil

1 teaspoon garlic powder

¼ teaspoon grated lemon zest

2 tablespoons freshly squeezed lemon juice

2 teaspoons freshly squeezed orange juice

3 teaspoons sea salt

1 teaspoon crushed black pepper

FOR THE SALAD

1 large bunch of kale, chopped (about 16 ounces)

2 small oranges, peeled and sectioned

1 grapefruit, peeled and sectioned

Pine nuts or other crunchy topping for serving

In a large bowl, whisk together the olive oil, garlic powder, lemon zest, lemon juice, orange juice, salt, and black pepper.

Add the chopped kale to the bowl and toss thoroughly with your hands to coat. Gently massage the kale leaves for 3 to 4 minutes, or until all the leaves are well coated with dressing and become slightly softer to the touch.

Allow to rest 3 to 5 minutes. Before serving, mix in the oranges and grapefruit. Toss lightly and top with pine nuts or your favorite crunchy topping.

Serve and enjoy!

PLANT PROPAGATION

The Gift
That Keeps on Giving

Propagation is the process of creating new plants from your existing plants and is a fun way to share the plant love in your home or with others. No matter how many times I propagate a new plant, I'm always shocked and delighted that it works. I'm like a proud mom: to me, each propagation is like a tiny green miracle.

There are a few different kinds of propagation, but the simplest and easiest to start with is water propagation. Water propagation involves taking a cutting of a mature plant and letting it take root in water until it grows roots and is ready to move into a pot with soil. It's that easy. I've had the best luck with pothos, ivy, pilea, monstera, and even fiddle-leaf figs. Here's how you can get started.

1. Choose the plant you will take your cutting from. Not all plants that root in water have nodes, the area on a stem where buds are located, but most of them do. So find a node on your plant, then carefully cut about one-quarter inch below the node with clean scissors.

2. Stick your new cutting into a clean glass filled with fresh room-temperature water. Make sure that the node—the place you just cut—is submerged.

3. The trick with water propagation is patience. I've had plants that didn't sprout roots for two months, then suddenly it happened. It can take weeks or months for your little propagated baby to start growing, so don't give up. Just when you're about to give up, you'll probably start to see new growth. Remember, good things come to those who wait!

4. Finally, after the roots are about five inches long, you can move the propagated plant into a pot of fresh nutrient-rich soil. Make sure to learn what kind of light and water this particular species of plant will need as it grows up. Once you know this, you can get into a routine of weekly care for your new little sprout and watch her grow, grow, grow until she herself is ready to be propagated.

Keep in mind that even if you follow all these steps carefully, propagation isn't always successful. There are a lot of factors that can work against you. So don't give up if your propagation fails a few times—that's pretty normal (it happened to me a lot when I started). But plants are surprisingly resilient. Just when you think one is dying, it will bounce back and grow for years, so just keep trying!

REFLECTION

Is there a dream for your life that you are afraid to pursue? If so, what is holding you back? And what would it take for you to step out of your comfort zone and chase your dream? Speak your dream aloud, write it down, tell a friend. Then make a practical plan to help you get going. Remember, even baby steps mean forward motion.

SWEET STRAWBERRY BASIL MULE

*There are a lot of variations on my favorite springtime cocktail—
the Moscow mule—but my favorite is all about handcrafting a naturally
fruity drink that is just a little bit tangy and a lotta bit refreshing.*

There are so many cocktails out there, and they all have funky names and special ingredients . . . but I like to keep it simple and stick with the two or three cocktails I know I love. And then, when I make one at home, of course, I have to do a little experimenting to make it my own.

Unlike other more alcohol-forward cocktails, the mule is all about the tasty mix-ins. So with that in mind, it's important to use really fresh ingredients when making this simple recipe.

With bright red strawberries, luscious green basil, freshly squeezed lime juice, and your favorite tangy ginger beer, you simply can't go wrong!

PREP TIME: 10 MINUTES

TOTAL TIME: 10 MINUTES

SERVES 1

6 fresh strawberries, stemmed and hulled

6 fresh basil leaves

¾ ounce freshly squeezed lime juice

2 ounces vodka

Crushed ice

2 to 3 ounces organic ginger beer

Lime slices for garnish

Place 5 strawberries and 5 basil leaves in the bottom of a cocktail shaker or mason jar with a tight-fitting lid.

Pour the lime juice on top, then muddle the fruit with the back of a spoon.

Add the vodka to the shaker and then a handful of ice. Cover and shake well.

Fill a tall glass with crushed ice and strain the mixture into the glass (a copper mug is traditional, but you can use whatever you've got!). Top with ginger beer.

Garnish with a sliced strawberry, basil leaf, and lime.

MAY

———

A SEASON
OF CREATION

MAY IS THE HARBINGER OF SUMMER—WITH long, warm, sunny days, it's a month that is all about converting the fresh energy of spring into something new, something creative.

Growing up, I did not think I was a very creative person. As a kid, I never tried to impress my family with stand-up comedy in the living room or with imaginative Lego and Play-Doh sculptures. I wasn't a great artist. I didn't act or sing or do ballet. For some people, creativity comes easily. But, for others, like me, discovering their unique creative instincts only happens through a process of discovery or trial and error. It can also happen through the process of developing and nurturing inspiring relationships.

My own creative instincts only started to come into focus after I left home and moved away to college. It was then that I started to understand that creativity can manifest itself in an almost infinite number of forms. Instead of making things, my creative awakening was about learning to set up spaces that encouraged certain kinds of feelings and experiences.

It all started when I realized that I could see physical spaces the way some people see blank canvases—something full of almost limitless potential just waiting to be un-locked and set free. First it happened in my tiny dorm room, then it happened again in the house I shared with my four best college girlfriends. I almost couldn't help myself. Every room where I spent any significant amount of time started to bother me in one way or another, challenging me—almost daring me—to try to make it cozier, brighter, more welcoming, or just simpler.

A room, like a canvas, is a defined space, which means there are natural limitations to what is possible. Every room has a certain number of walls and windows and square feet, and this is a good thing, because projects without rules or limitations feel chaotic to me, and I can get easily overwhelmed with too much choice and give up. So conceptualizing rooms as blank canvases feels natural and manageable.

Right away, I discovered that if I added a fresh coat of paint to the walls, put new linens in neutral colors on the bed, arranged a nice plant or two near the window, and propped up a few pieces of minimalist art (even homemade or thrift-shop art) on a table, a space could feel entirely different: cleaner, warmer, more relaxing, more inviting. Best of all, approaching interiors this way was also pretty inexpensive (I was still a student, after all).

Pretty soon, I found that my friends and roommates started spending an increasing amount of time in my room: hanging out, studying, and coming in to have long chats. Before I fully knew what was happening, my friends started to encourage and praise my newfound creative impulses. The reality is that I didn't know anything about architecture or interior design or decorating. I was just trying to create a new kind of feeling in these little rented sanctuaries where I was learning to be an adult.

After Marcus and I got married and moved into our house in LA, the challenge was much bigger: instead of one room in a rented house, there was an entire home to consider. But working from room to room, space to space, I continued to follow my gut. I tried things out, moved things around, and created a loose set of aesthetic values: less plastic, more plants; hide storage whenever possible; emphasize neutral colors; seek out simple, timeless (often thrifted) furniture.

Throughout, Marcus was supportive and often weighed in when we needed to make decisions together, but homemaking isn't really one of his serious creative interests. So the task of converting that basically generic space—that big blank canvas—into a cozy home perfect for us fell to me. During this process, I learned so much about myself and what I want from the spaces where I live. Ever since, my creativity has continued to grow and evolve. And I hope it always will!

Obviously, as life changes come along, your space needs change as well: an office becomes a baby room, then later it becomes a kid's room, and one day—who knows?—a wall comes down and that same room becomes part of an expanded living space. A house is a creative playground for me: thinking this way helps keep me on my toes and looking to the future. It's both practical and imaginative. And sometimes, the possibilities seem endless. If I'm not careful, I can easily spiral down the rabbit hole of what-ifs. What if we covered that wall entirely in plants? What if I painted constellations on the ceiling of James's room? What if our kitchen table was made of a giant slab of bleached driftwood? Where does one even find a giant slab of bleached driftwood? Of course, this is half the fun of any creative endeavor, right? Wondering, dreaming, imagining the potential.

In my experience, the common thread that connects all creative efforts—no matter the size or shape of the project—is an open heart and an open mind. Sure, being creative requires a certain amount of skill and experience, but it also demands a certain amount of openness, to see what will happen if we try something we haven't done before. Creativity is the beautiful balancing act of using what we know combined with a kind of naive curiosity, a desire to try something just beyond our current skill set. Living a creative life might be as simple as being willing to say yes to something before fully understanding how the heck you're going to pull it off.

Growing in creativity doesn't mean trying to go out and create a masterpiece as soon as you finish reading this page. Instead, it's mostly about consciously deciding to be actively involved in shaping some aspect of the world around you. Of course, that can be through artistic pursuits like painting or writing a novel or playing music. But creativity is not the same as artistic ability. It begins somewhere deep inside each of us and then manifests itself as something outward, from the ways we express emotion to the ways we raise our kids or support our partners or get involved in our communities. We could probably come up with a million creative ideas for making a positive impact. Some of us would start with music, others with food, others with storytelling, others with history or poetry or landscaping or home design. There is no one right answer. There is creative energy in all these methods, just as there is a creative spirit at work in each of us, showing itself in a thousand little ways throughout our daily lives.

The point is, you are creative. You have the ability to add value and beauty and meaning to the world through your ideas, passion, and the ways you touch others each and every day. So what are you waiting for? Go and make something beautiful today.

REFLECTION

Is there something you have created that gives you a sense of meaning or joy? Is there room for you to be more creative in your daily life? If there is something holding you back, what would it take to remove that obstacle?

LOUISIANA CRAWFISH BOIL

A genuine Louisiana-style crawfish boil is a blast—a big, social, messy, one-of-a-kind event that you have to try at least once in your life. Trust me: you'll never forget it. But even if you can't make it to New Orleans for a proper boil, don't worry. This recipe will help you bring this quintessential Cajun experience into your home or backyard. Just make sure there are plenty of ice-cold drinks on hand!

If you've never been to a Louisiana crawfish boil, you have to imagine a kind of backyard barbecue where you get together to boil crustaceans (alive!) in a giant pot of spicy broth and then, as soon as they're ready, dump them all onto a picnic table covered with newspaper and go nuts, elbow to elbow with friends and family, happily shelling and eating this spicy delicacy with your bare hands until all that's left is a mountain of shells and a very happy crowd. To the uninitiated, it might sound barbaric. But to me, it's just about my all-time favorite memory of childhood: all the sights and sounds, the extended family gathered together, and the fragrant smell of Cajun spices filling the early summer air. It's just so nostalgic!

These days, it can be difficult for us to get our hands on fresh crawfish now that we don't live in Louisiana anymore. But I'm committed to keeping the tradition alive. For our family, it's well worth the extra effort and expense to invest in a big crawfish boil once a year. It's a non-negotiable event at our house that I will take with me no matter where we live. Thanks to the internet, there are now some good options for obtaining fresh crawfish, shipped alive overnight, so that no matter where you live in the United States, you can probably make a real boil happen if you're willing and able. Keep in mind that crawfish season varies from year to year depending on the weather along the Gulf Coast. But typically, the biggest and best-quality crawfish are available from March to May each year, so keep that in mind when you're planning your boil.

The recipe that follows is a modified version of the big family crawfish boils I described above. This one can be prepared outside if you have the right setup for it, but it's also easy to pull off in your kitchen. No matter where you cook your "mudbugs," though, it's best to eat them outside, where cleanup is easiest. Besides, a crawfish boil always tastes better with the sun on your face and the wind in your hair.

Actually, you should tie back that hair. Things are about to get real messy!

PREP TIME: 20 MINUTES

COOK TIME: 1 TO 2 HOURS

TOTAL TIME: 2½ HOURS

SERVES 8

8 cloves garlic

2½ cups Old Bay seasoning

5 cups CeCe's Cajun Seasoning (page 47)

2 lemons, quartered

4 ears of corn, each shucked and cut into 4-inch pieces

1 pound small red potatoes, halved

1 onion, peeled and sliced into wedges

1 pound andouille sausage, sliced in 1-inch pieces

30 pounds fresh, rinsed live crawfish in their shells

1 cup (2 sticks) melted butter for serving

Fill a large pot just over half full with water and set over medium-high heat.

Add the garlic, Old Bay and Cajun seasoning, and lemons. Bring to a boil.

Add the corn and potatoes. Boil for about 10 minutes, or until the potatoes are soft.

Add the onion and sausage. Cover and boil for 5 more minutes.

Gently stir in the crawfish. Boil for 5 to 6 minutes, or until the crawfish turn bright red.

Drain the crawfish.

Transfer the crawfish and vegetables to a large serving platter or simply pour everything out onto a tabletop covered in newspaper—this is the old-school style and the way we do it at my mom and dad's house. Place ramekins of melted butter around the table for dipping.

Get busy feasting!

THE BEAUTY OF IMPERFECTION

Rustic Hand-Dyed Linens

I've found that working with my hands—whether I'm baking, building something, or brewing kombucha—involves a number of interesting and challenging steps. From the moment I'm exposed to a new idea until the moment I create something for the first time, I am engaging in a number of activities, including research, collection, preparation, experimentation, collaboration, and practice, practice, practice. Along the way, I learn a lot by doing, and inevitably, I have quite a few false starts and stumbles along the way. But that's a big part of being creative; mistakes and imperfections are part of the journey.

A great example of this is hand-dying fabrics. Did you know that you can dye fabrics with onion skins? This is a fun and beautiful way to create something special, and the best part is, it's very forgiving, so it's easy to do.

Because you're working with natural fabrics and natural dyes, the whole endeavor is very organic in the sense that it isn't ever going to be a perfect process. The results will probably vary widely depending on the ratio of onion skin to water, the temperature and pH of the dye bath, the fabric you use, and your level of experience.

If you mess up, that's okay: no two hand-dyed fabrics will ever look exactly the same, and that's the beauty of dyeing by hand. Every batch of onions will produce a slightly different color, from pastel grays to shades of sun-washed rose to rich violet tones. So don't be afraid to mess up. Instead, lean in to every part of this creative learning process. You might discover a new passion or talent you never knew you had.

WHAT YOU'LL NEED

1 12 x 12-inch piece of nonsynthetic fabric, such as linen or cotton

1 8- to 10-quart stainless steel cooking pot with lid

Water

Red or brown onion skins from 10 to 12 yellow, white, or red onions

1 bucket the same size as or bigger than the cooking pot

1 piece of muslin big enough to cover the mouth of the bucket

Strong elastic band big enough to fit around the bucket

Stainless steel tongs or stainless steel or wooden spoon

Before you start, run the fabric that you want to dye through the rinse cycle of your washing machine in cold water *without* adding any detergent, fabric softener, or other clothes (unless you will be dyeing those as well). This step will remove impurities on the fabric and help it absorb the pigment.

1. While the fabric is in the machine, fill your cooking pot with enough water to cover the fabric yet allow it to move about freely.

2. Place the pot on the stove and bring the water to a boil. Add the onion skins, reduce to a simmer, and cover.

3. Allow the skins to simmer for 1 to 1½ hours, until the water changes to the desired color. Keep in mind that the longer the skins "cook," the darker the dye bath will be. You can basically boil the onion skins until they turn to mush.

4. Once you're happy with the color of the water, remove the pot from the heat. Cover the top of the bucket with the muslin and strain the dye bath from the pot into the bucket. This helps achieve an even distribution of pigment. Enlist another set of hands for this step if you can. Otherwise, use an elastic band to strap down the muslin before straining. Toss the skins into the trash or compost bin.

5. Remove any remaining solids from the pot, remove the muslin from the bucket, and pour the strained dye back into the pot.

6. Return the pot to low heat.

7. Add the fabric that you want to dye to the dye bath in the pot; make sure it is still thoroughly damp from the washing machine. Using stainless steel tongs or a spoon, stir the fabric until it's completely immersed.

⟶

8. Allow the fabric to rest in the dye bath for about 1 to 1½ hours, stirring occasionally. Keep the heat low.

9. When you're happy with the fabric color, carefully remove it from the dye bath using the tongs and hang it to dry overnight somewhere it can drip without damaging the flooring (outside is best, but not in direct sunlight). Keep in mind that the fabric will lighten as it dries, so don't remove it from the dye bath too soon.

10. You can use your dye bath again, but the second batch of fabric will be lighter in color.

11. The next day, iron your newly dyed fabrics on low heat to help set the color.

12. Rinse the newly dyed fabrics with cool water (to prevent colors bleeding) and hang again to dry.

TIPS

Approximately 30 grams of onion skins will provide strong color for 100 grams or a 12 x 12-inch piece of fabric.

Consider wearing a disposable mask and gloves while working closely with dyes. Even though the process is all natural, exposure might irritate some people with sensitivities.

It's best not to use your everyday cooking pots for your dyeing project, because the metal can stain or change color. I recommend buying some inexpensive stainless steel tools (pot, lid, tongs, spoon) at a thrift store, then keeping them separate from the equipment you use for food. When you're done with your dyeing project, store these items away from the kitchen area.

You can machine-wash dyed fabrics in cool water on the gentle cycle and hang to air dry.

LAVENDER BLACKBERRY LAYER CAKE

*Everybody loves cake—the perfect sweet treat to celebrate a special
person or occasion. A homemade cake is like a beautiful, delicious gift
that you get to decorate, give away, and then eat. What could be better?*

I love making food for people. I find it really satisfying to engage my creativity by learning the
tools and tricks of the trade, adapting recipes, and creating something with my hands that
friends and family will enjoy.

Making a cake feels like an extra-special act of love. This particular lavender blackberry
layer cake is at once complex and simple, rustic and refined, decadent and light as a feather. It
brings together floral flavors, earthy berries, and rich buttery goodness. Plus, it's so pretty!

I've made this layer cake for friends on several occasions, and it always seems to be well
received. I mean, there are never any leftovers . . . and I guess that's the true test of any recipe!

PREP TIME: 45 MINUTES

COOK TIME: 30 MINUTES

TOTAL TIME: 1¼ HOURS

SERVES 10

FOR THE CAKE

3 cups all-purpose flour

1 teaspoon fine kosher salt

2½ teaspoons baking
powder

1⅓ cups buttermilk

½ cup vegetable oil

2 tablespoons vanilla
extract

TO MAKE THE CAKE

Preheat the oven to 350°F.

Line the bottoms of two 9-inch round cake pans with parchment paper.

In a large mixing bowl, whisk together the flour, salt, and baking powder. Set aside.

In a medium bowl, whisk together the buttermilk, oil, and vanilla extract. Set aside.

In the bowl of a stand mixer fitted with the paddle attachment, beat the butter on low speed for 3 minutes. Gradually add the granulated sugar.

Increase the speed to medium and mix for another 3 to 5 minutes, until the mixture is light and fluffy.

———→

½ cup (1 stick) unsalted butter, at room temperature

1½ cups granulated sugar

4 large eggs, at room temperature

FOR THE COMPOTE

5 cups fresh blackberries

2 teaspoons culinary lavender

1 cup granulated sugar

1 cup water

FOR THE FROSTING

8 ounces cream cheese, at room temperature

1 cup (2 sticks) unsalted butter, at room temperature

½ teaspoon fine kosher salt

2 teaspoons vanilla extract

3 to 5 cups confectioners' sugar

FOR GARNISH

Blackberries

Flowers

Sprigs of rosemary

Fresh mint

Lemon slices

Mix in the eggs one at a time.

Reduce the speed to low. Add a third of the dry ingredients, followed by half the buttermilk mixture. Add another third of the dry ingredients, followed by the remaining half of the buttermilk mixture. Blend in the remaining dry ingredients. Mix each element until only just combined.

Evenly divide the mixture between the prepared cake pans.

Bake for 25 to 30 minutes, or until a toothpick inserted into the center comes out clean. Remove from the oven and allow cakes to cool in the pans for about 20 minutes.

Turn the cakes out onto a cooling rack and allow to cool for another hour. (At this point, the cakes can be wrapped tightly and frozen overnight for easy decorating. They can be stored for up to 3 months in the freezer!)

TO MAKE THE COMPOTE

While the cakes are cooling, combine the blackberries, lavender, sugar, and water in a saucepan and bring to a boil.

Reduce the heat to a simmer and cook for about 15 minutes, stirring regularly. Use a wooden spoon to break down the blackberries.

After the mixture has thickened and reduced by half, transfer it to a glass container. Allow it to cool, then cover tightly and refrigerate until thickened, about an hour. (The compote can be prepared up to a week ahead of time and stored in the refrigerator).

TO MAKE THE FROSTING

Combine the cream cheese and butter in the bowl of a stand mixer fitted with the paddle attachment and beat until creamy. (You can also use an electric hand mixer.)

Add the salt and vanilla extract and mix well.

Reduce the mixer speed to low and gradually add the confectioners' sugar until completely combined.

TO ASSEMBLE

Once everything is prepared and the cakes are both cooled to room temperature, you're ready to assemble this beauty. To make a four-layer cake, cut each cake in half horizontally. (Or, for a two-layer cake, you can simply leave the layers whole.)

Place a dollop of frosting onto a cake stand and lay your first layer on top, rounded side down. Cover the top with frosting.

Next, add a few spoonfuls of the berry compote on top of the frosting (it's okay if it drips down the sides a little).

Add your next cake layer on top and frost.

Repeat the layers in order: cake, frosting, compote, then when you've placed the top layer of cake, ice the top and sides of the entire cake.

Garnish the cake with fresh blackberries, flowers, sprigs of rosemary or mint, lemon slices, or anything else you have on hand. I love getting creative with this part! Slice and enjoy.

JUNE

———

A SEASON FOR ADVENTURE

I AM MARRIED TO A VERY ADVENTUROUS man. And when I say "very adventurous," I mean *very* adventurous (like, sometimes I worry). On any given day, Marcus can be found chopping down trees, swimming in a river, climbing something, or demolishing or building something. Seriously—it never ends for him. As I write this, I'm almost certain Marcus is outside somewhere not too far off, covered in a combination of sweat, mud, gear grease, and dog slobber. And he's happy as can be.

Here's a sampling of just a few of the adventurous things Marcus has done since I've known him (I do not recommend or condone any of these, by the way).

- Camping in Yosemite National Park in subzero weather

- Floating down an alligator-infested creek in Florida on a pink pool float

- Off-roading in the mountains in a tiny 1994 Geo Tracker that we bought for $900

- Crashing an old junker car in the desert to get an amazing slow-motion shot of the car flipping over

- Sneaking onto some boxcars with a few friends and riding the trains around

the Pacific Northwest just for fun . . . until they got arrested

- Trying to teach me to drive a stick shift (maybe the riskiest of all!)

See what I mean? This boy has got wildness in his blood!

As for me . . . not so much. I also like to have adventures, but I can assure you that you will never find me rafting down a river on a pool float or jumping onto moving freight cars. I'm good, thanks. I'll watch the videos after. But hey, I'm still fun! I can even be spontaneous, and I'm pretty outdoorsy-ish for a homebody. In fact, being outdoors helps remind me just how big and beautiful the world is and how relatively small we are. Whether you're at the beach or in the mountains or simply standing under the shade of a one-hundred-year-old oak tree in your local park, nature has the power to humble and inspire at the same time. And sometimes we have to venture out of our comfort zones to experience its full power. I know I do.

Once, I was invited on a trip to the Rocky Mountains. It was a minimally rustic trip, but my girlfriends and I were planning on pushing ourselves by taking some challenging hikes. At some point, someone posed a question: What if we did a predawn hike so that we could watch the sunrise over the mountains?

None of us had done anything like that before. We didn't even know if it was possible. But our host and guide told us that it was possible and that she would lead us if we wanted to go. It seemed dangerous. Perhaps even foolish. But it also sounded amazing. We decided to go for it. And what started out as a whim would turn out to be one of the most adventurous, challenging, and wonderful experiences of my life.

Our guide woke us at 3:00 a.m. Normally, this would not be my kind of thing: climbing out of a warm sleeping bag five hours early just to stumble up a mountain in the cold dark while semiconscious? Um, no thanks. But if we wanted to reach the summit by sunrise, around 6:00 a.m., we had to start early. We threw on clothes and boots, and chugged coffee before setting out into the dark morning.

The hike was hard. Like, so hard. I'm pretty sure I cried more than once, actually. Not only did the hike include a lot of bouldering and places where we had to crawl on all fours, we also had to keep a brisk pace so we wouldn't miss the sunrise. What I remember most about those predawn hours was feeling pretty disoriented and being in a pretty bad mood. Except for little bursts of encouragement on especially difficult patches of the path, our group was quiet all the way up the mountain. Nobody really felt like talking, and we needed to focus all our attention on the unlit path.

Then, after hours of walking through the dark, tripping over roots, stumbling over one another, and sweating despite the cold morning, we finally made it to the top of the mountain. Exhausted but happy to have survived the hike up, everyone spread out and found places to sit and catch their breath. We actually arrived at the summit a little bit early, so we had time to sip water, munch on granola bars, chat, and complain and laugh quietly. For some reason, we all felt like whispering. For what seemed like a long time, we stared off into the east, waiting to watch the world wake up.

First we noticed the sky change from indigo to violet. Then the mountains to the east were suddenly silhouetted by a climbing golden halo. Finally, it happened: the sun rose up over the horizon, and darkness was overwhelmed by the warm white light of morning. Below us, mountains and forests and rivers were suddenly visible, the whole living world lush and green and alive. Nobody spoke for a long time. What could we even say? It was all so breathtaking. So we just sat there, watching the sky change colors and the whole world around us become illuminated by the light of a brand-new day.

We all pulled out our phones to document the gorgeous sunrise, only to realize later that our photos couldn't capture the magic of that mountaintop moment. Not really. They were beautiful snapshots, yes, souvenirs of a truly amazing experience. But they didn't tell the whole story. Photos rarely do, I suppose. I guess you just had to be there. I'm certainly glad I was. It was one of the most unforgettable experiences of my life, a true treasure.

I think the reason this experience is so precious to me is because it helped me see something new in both the natural world and in myself. Before that day in Colorado, I had never woken up at 3:00 a.m. on purpose. I had never climbed a mountain in the dark, and I had certainly never watched a sunrise from nine thousand feet above sea level. I was both physically and emotionally challenged by that sunrise hike and spiritually rewarded in a deep and profound way. For me, this is one of the most beautiful things about nature: it can challenge us and, at the same time, comfort and center us.

Nothing helps calm me in quite the same way as spending time outside. In LA, whenever life felt like it was just too much or I needed to clear my head, I'd head to one of the beautiful hiking trails around the city to get out of the house and into the sunshine. During those hikes, whether with my girlfriends or with my dogs, I'd get some exercise and reset emotionally and mentally. Those walks were like free therapy, honestly.

Today, life looks a lot different. We've traded the Hollywood Hills for the foothills of the Great Smoky Mountains, here in Tennessee. And though the stresses of life are somewhat different, my favorite method of self-care is still the same: I go outside. It just makes me feel better. And think better. And be a better version of myself. No matter how busy I am, I try to make time to walk in nature most days. With Marcus, with James, with the dogs, or alone—it doesn't matter. These walks may not pack the same sublime spiritual punch as witnessing a mountaintop sunrise, but they're still very, very good for my soul. I truly believe that almost any time in nature is time well spent.

Luckily, we don't have to be up at 3:00 a.m. to benefit from the many wonders of nature. The natural world is there 24–7, and there are countless adventures just waiting to be had. All we have to do is step outside.

MOM'S FAMOUS
BARBECUE BABY BACK RIBS

Getting out into nature can be as easy as having a backyard barbecue,
and these delicious baby back ribs are the heart and soul of
my all-time favorite barbecue meal.

One of the best parts of summertime is enjoying the outdoors, and grilling and barbecuing are a great way to soak up the sunshine. When I was growing up, my mom would make these incredible baby back ribs that we'd devour on hot summer days, and one year, for the Fourth of July, I decided to try my hand at making them for the first time.

I was nine months pregnant with James, and despite my rule of never cooking a new-to-me recipe for guests, I was, in fact, cooking these ribs for Marcus's whole family. Would it have been easier to do burgers or have barbecue delivered? Sure it would have. But despite being ultra pregnant, I would not be deterred: I was finally going to learn how to make my mom's famous barbecue baby back ribs.

Around ten minutes in, though, I realized that I needed backup. Luckily, I had my mom on speed dial that weekend. I must have called her a dozen times during the process, from my trip to the butcher shop all the way through to the end. As always, she was there when I needed her! She very patiently walked me through each of the steps so that I felt confident enough to serve these ribs to my very hungry family. With Mom's help, I pulled it off, watching the ribs quickly disappear. I guess that's why they're so famous! By the way, make sure there are plenty of napkins on the table for this messy, delicious meal.

PREP TIME: 30 MINUTES

COOK TIME: 3 HOURS

TOTAL TIME: 3½ HOURS

SERVES 8

FOR THE RUB

2½ tablespoons smoked paprika

½ teaspoon cayenne pepper

½ tablespoon freshly ground black pepper

2½ tablespoons garlic powder

3 tablespoons onion powder

1 tablespoon kosher salt

2 teaspoons dried oregano

2 teaspoons dried thyme

FOR THE RIBS

4 racks baby back ribs or St. Louis ribs (ask your butcher to remove the silverskin)

4 tablespoons olive oil

¼ cup liquid smoke mixed with 1 tablespoon water

2 cups prepared barbecue sauce

Preheat the oven to 300°F.

Combine the paprika, cayenne, pepper, garlic powder, onion powder, salt, oregano, and thyme in a small bowl.

Line two large baking sheets with foil, leaving a 6-inch overhang on each of the long sides and a 3-inch overhang on each of the short sides. Place the ribs on the foil with the meat side up.

Lightly coat the ribs with olive oil (this will help the rub stick).

Using your hands, generously coat the ribs on both sides with the spice rub.

Divide the liquid smoke mixture between two small oven-safe bowls or ramekins, each approximately 3 inches in diameter. Place the bowls beside the ribs on top of the foil.

Fold over the foil so that it covers the ribs and bowls tightly. Make sure you can open the foil at the top after cooking.

Cook for 2½ to 3 hours. Do not open the oven door while cooking.

Remove the baking sheets from the oven, open the foil at the top, and brush the ribs with barbecue sauce. Fold over the foil again and seal tightly to cover. Preheat the broiler to high.

Broil the ribs for 3 to 5 minutes, or until the barbecue sauce gets caramelized. Watch closely to avoid burning.

Serve with your favorite summertime sides, including potato salad, coleslaw, baked beans, and Texas toast.

A WALK IN THE WOODS

Decorating with
Found Natural Objects

Every walk in the woods or trip to the river becomes a kind of treasure hunt when you realize you can use almost everything around you to create a connection with nature in your home. What will I find today? Aren't these stones interesting? Isn't this driftwood amazing? Won't that pinecone look cool up on a shelf?

One way I create a sense of calm in my home is through the use of these natural found objects. You can call it salvaging or collecting, but whatever term you choose, the idea is simple: use the beauty and diversity of nature in an artful way, helping bring the peacefulness of nature indoors. Depending on where you live (and where you travel!), you will have access to various kinds of wood, driftwood, plants, flowers, stones, sand, soil. . . . The list is endless.

To help you get started, I've shared some ideas for a few ways I like to use found natural objects. Plus, once I started working with organic materials in this way, I looked at nature and the changing seasons in a whole new light.

MEMORY JARS

I got this idea from my nephew, Owen, who is a master collector. Whenever he and his parents go on a beach vacation, they take along a mason jar and carefully collect the "best" small beach stones they can find. Once the jar is full, the project is finished. Then, when they get home, they label the jar with the name of the beach and the date and place it on a shelf where they can see it and remember the trip together.

DRIFTWOOD PHOTO GALLERY WALL

Years ago, when I was living at my parents' house, I did a full-on renovation of my childhood bedroom and came up with the idea of making a driftwood wall hanging that could function as an anchor for a kind of hanging photo gallery. I got a piece of wood from the beach, and I used some natural twine and a few wooden clothespins to create something like a mobile, so that the photos hung down from this beautiful, sculptural piece of driftwood.

BIG BOWL FULL OF SHELLS

When we lived in LA, we had a friend who collected all kinds of seashells: big shells; small shells; spiky, shiny, matte, colorful, and neutral shells. She kept them in a large wooden bowl in her living room, and I noticed that anytime people came over to hang out, they would inevitably want to touch, hold, and pass the shells around. It was a great conversation starter . . . and I think it's time I started my own collection to bring a little LA beachiness to our Nashville home!

MIX-AND-MATCH EARTHENWARE PLANTERS

Chances are, no matter where you live, you won't have to look very hard to find vintage terra-cotta and ceramic planters at thrift shops and garage sales. They're everywhere! And while these items aren't, strictly speaking, natural found objects, they are made from a simple, natural material—clay—that comes in countless colors and textures. Try mixing and matching various sizes, shapes, and types of planters to create an earthy green space somewhere in your home, whether on a set of shelves, pressed up against a large window, or in a cozy corner space.

DRIED PLANTS AS SCULPTURE

Besides pressing wildflowers and making them into framed art (see page 155), another way to celebrate the wild, organic beauty of plants is to dry them naturally and allow them to stand alone on a table or shelf as pieces of natural sculpture. Eucalyptus is one plant that dries beautifully and looks lacy and dramatic—and often smells amazing, too!

ANTLERS

I am not a hunter. No judgment of people who hang animal heads on their walls—I just think I'd be creeped out by the dead Bambi eyes following me around while I Swiffer in my Saturday sweats. Antlers, however, are super beautiful and interesting to look at and touch. You can sometimes find boxes of old antlers at flea markets, so keep your eye out. Or if you know a hunter, he or she may have some to give you or sell to you. Hang them on a wall or arrange them on a shelf as a focal point. However you use antlers in the home, they add a really nice sculptural element to any space.

A WREATH FOR EVERY SEASON

Using plants, flowers, and even grasses or vines, you can create gorgeous wreaths appropriate for all seasons. The availability of plants and flowers will obviously vary, but do some research and experiment with what will work best for your region and the time of year. Tip: use something relatively hardy for the base of your wreath, because if you use something too soft, such as willow branches, you'll likely end up with a soggy, saggy mess sliding down the wall.

FIREWOOD STACKS

Okay, so by now, you probably know that I love things that are neat and tidy. Not only do I feel calmed by order, I also find it very beautiful. So that means I actually get aesthetic joy from a neatly stacked pile of firewood (I know—total nerd!). Anyway, if you look around on Pinterest and Instagram, you will find all sorts of cool ways that people have incorporated a neat stack of firewood into their interior designs. It can be used as a room divider, stored under a bench, or even function as a kind of textural freestanding art. Just watch out for bugs and critters sneaking into your stack.

MINIATURE KEY LIME PIES

*How do you make the most refreshing summer dessert in the world
even more delicious? Easy: you make it tiny and adorable.
This recipe for miniature Key lime pies is inspired by my Florida roots
and is guaranteed to satisfy your summer sweet tooth.*

When I was a kid, my family moved from Louisiana to Florida, where my dad is from. Each time I visit the Florida Keys, I'm reminded that the southernmost tip of America is a strange and special place, almost like another country—wild and tropical and remote. But for me, the highlight of every trip to the Keys isn't snorkeling in the crystal-clear water or exploring the lovely landscape: it's the food. Specifically, the specialty that the Keys are most famous for: Key lime pie.

Key lime pie is both light and decadent, fruity and buttery, refreshing and substantial. Served cold, it's the perfect summertime treat. If you can't get to the Keys, eating this pie is maybe the next best thing. This particular recipe is a twist on my dad's, which has been tweaked and perfected over the years. I've made it my own by making the pies miniature and adorable, and since then, I've tested this recipe on my dad, who, I'm proud to say, has given it a true Floridian's stamp of approval.

PREP TIME: 20 MINUTES

COOK TIME: 20 TO 25 MINUTES

TOTAL TIME: 45 MINUTES

SERVES 8 TO 10

FOR THE CRUST

1½ cups crushed graham crackers

¼ cup granulated sugar

Preheat the oven to 350°F.

In the bowl of a food processor or blender, combine the graham crackers and sugar, and process until the graham crackers form fine crumbs.

Add the butter and pulse until well mixed. If you pull out a chunk and smoosh it between your fingers, it should hold together.

Coat a standard-size muffin tin with nonstick cooking spray.

Using a spoon or your fingers, press the crumb mixture firmly onto the bottom and sides of the cups.

⟶

5 tablespoons unsalted
butter, melted

Nonstick cooking spray

FOR THE FILLING

1 14-ounce can sweetened
condensed milk

4 large egg yolks

½ cup freshly squeezed
lime juice, preferably from
Key limes, strained

1 teaspoon lime zest, plus
extra for garnish

FOR THE TOPPING

½ cup heavy whipping
cream

2 tablespoons
confectioners' sugar

¼ teaspoon vanilla extract

Lime slices for garnish

Bake for 8 minutes, or until lightly browned.

Remove from the oven and cool while preparing the filling.

In a medium bowl, whisk together the sweetened condensed milk and egg yolks until smooth. Add the lime juice and zest and whisk until blended. Pour the filling into the cooled crusts and bake for 12 to 15 minutes, or until set (the filling shouldn't move around when shaken).

Remove the pies from the tin and place on a cooling rack. Allow to set fully and cool to room temperature.

Refrigerate several hours or overnight before serving.

Just before serving, make the topping: beat the heavy cream until soft peaks form. Add the confectioners' sugar and vanilla, and beat until stiff but still a little soft. Using a spoon or pastry bag, top each pie with the whipped cream. Garnish with lime zest and a thin slice of lime.

REFLECTION

First Lady Eleanor Roosevelt once said, "The purpose of life, after all, is to live it, to taste experience to the utmost, to reach out eagerly and without fear for a newer and richer experience." What is a personal, professional, or relational adventure that you'd like to embark on during this season of life?

———

A SEASON
OF DISCOVERY

FOR MANY PEOPLE, MYSELF INCLUDED, THE arrival of summer means it's time to travel. Whether it's because the kids have a break from school or because it's easier to sightsee when it's warm and sunny, summer is the perfect time for taking a trip. And it's hard for me to think of anything that has helped me grow more than travel.

I am so grateful that I was born into a family that could and did make travel a priority for us when we were little kids. I know this isn't always possible for everyone, but my mom and dad were committed to making two trips happen for our family each year: a ski trip during the winter and each summer a trip to the beach in Florida, where my dad is from. We looked forward to these special trips all year long and dreamed about winter days spent high up in the magical mountains and summer days spent splashing in tide pools and burying our parents' feet in little hills of golden sand.

Looking back now, I know that making those trips happen couldn't have been easy for my mom and dad. There was the expense, of course, but also the inevitable inconvenience of it all: the delayed flights and long drives, the stubborn snowsuits and bundles of beach gear, the car sickness and back-seat brawling and, of course, the unpredictable weather. Honestly, it's a wonder my parents kept it up all those years while remaining relatively calm. And yet they did it for us. It was a priority for them. And, I think, a pleasure, too. Now, with a little distance, I've come to understand why they placed so much importance on these trips year in and year out.

Those trips weren't only about getting away for a family vacation (traveling with little kids, especially, is never "a day at the beach," even when you are at the beach). They were also about exposing my sister and me to the world beyond our little hometown of Baton Rouge, Louisiana. We faced all kinds of logistical and emotional challenges along the way, and that was part of the experience—the adventure—of travel.

I remember the fun, of course—the snowball fights and giant ice cream cones—but in hindsight, it was through those childhood travels that I remember experiencing new landscapes and places, new people whose accents and foods and cultures were different from my own. Through travel, my parents were giving my sister and me a skill set that would help us later in life: the ability to manage adversity—to remain flexible when plans change or the weather is uncooperative, to solve problems on the go, to live without the little comforts of home, to be open to the unknown, and to do all this with a smile . . . or at least without too much moaning and groaning. These experiences boosted my confidence and made me curious about other people and places. I guess you could say my parents planted the seeds of wanderlust in my life.

Marcus and I have had so many wonderful opportunities to indulge that wanderlust, both around the United States and abroad. Switzerland, Greece, Italy, Spain, Morocco, Denmark—every single trip has been full of its own unique challenges and joys, and my memories of each are so meaningful. These trips have fostered some of our deepest bonding experiences as a couple, especially when we've had to make careful plans, overcome unexpected obstacles, and tolerate any number of travel inconveniences. One of the reasons Marcus decided to propose to me in Italy was because travel had become so important to us. It just felt right to him to connect that momentous occasion to a travel memory.

Once, while we were in Greece, someone messaged me and said that we made international travel look "so perfect and easy." And sure: on Instagram, everything looks easy, right? The colorful buildings, the shimmering sea, the summer dresses and sun-kissed skin. But the truth is that what you couldn't see on Instagram was

Marcus's lost luggage, the flight in Frankfurt that we missed, the debit card that would never work, the exasperated bickering, and the jet lag. Those things were also part of that same trip.

Frankly, there have been hard, annoying, and/or frustrating moments in every day we've spent traveling together, whether on a simple road trip to North Carolina or on a monthlong adventure in Europe. That's just reality. It may not show up on social media, but it's always there.

I'd guess struggle of one kind or another is pretty much the common denominator for travel experiences of every shape and size. Why? Because travel, by definition, is a *leaving* experience. A moving, a going away, a changing kind of experience. I've heard it said that travel is 50 percent pleasure and 50 percent pain, and I think that's about right. But in my experience, there's value in both the pleasure and the pain. The fun, photogenic memories represent the pleasure part—the joy—and that's what we remember fondly, what stays in our consciousness when we tell our favorite stories about our favorite trips.

But the pain part of travel also has a kind of value—a pushing, pulling, stretching, growing kind of value. Whenever we step out of our comfort zone, we are testing ourselves. We're willingly trying to see how we handle change, newness, and discomfort. In this way, the world can be a kind of big, beautiful obstacle course. Sure, it can be difficult to navigate and find our way, but it can also be infinitely rewarding. What unexpected experience will I find?

For example, I travel to Italy knowing that I will eat great food. That's largely why I want to go! What I don't know before I get there, though, is that on a quiet side street in Rome, not far from the Colosseum, there is a family-run trattoria that serves cacio e pepe, a pasta dish made with rich cheese and tons of freshly ground black pepper. Before I stumble upon this quaint place, I can't know that cacio e pepe will become my new favorite pasta dish of all time. Before I get there, I can't know that the kind old woman who runs the restaurant will invite me into her kitchen so I can see how she makes this sublimely simple dish. I can't know that she will take the time to show me the exact kind of peppercorns to use and the specific way she grates the cheese and how to best plate the pasta.

Before I get to Morocco, I can't know that I will have to sprint through the har-

bor in Tangier, trying to catch the last ferry back to Spain. I can't know that, on the Rock of Gibraltar, wild monkeys will play with my hair and eat bananas right out of my hand. Until I get to Copenhagen, I can't know that there is nothing quite like a warm Danish pastry right out of the oven. I can't know that I will experience any of this until I actually go out into the world with an open heart, ready to be surprised, to see and touch and taste and learn. I never know exactly what will happen until I go. None of us does. And that's the beauty of it all. We don't know until we go.

Then we come home changed—richer in experiences and memories and, we hope, a little bit stronger and more sure of ourselves. When we travel, we add these experiences and memories to our lives. And if we're lucky, we might even come home with a few new recipes that we learned from a real Italian grandma.

We just never know . . . until we go. And when we go, we almost always grow. For me, that kind of gain is well worth the pain.

TANGY RASPBERRY ALMOND GALETTE

*Fresh berries are almost impossible to beat. But this recipe for
a tangy raspberry galette has the advantage of combining the
bright tanginess of raspberries with another favorite treat of mine:
a rich, crumbly, buttery crust. This pairing takes the natural
goodness of raspberries to a whole new level.*

One of my fondest memories of summer goes back to 2016, when I was visiting my sister in Denmark. Her family was living in the countryside north of Copenhagen at the time, and since the weather was so nice, she and I took a lot of long walks together. And everywhere we went, we saw fruit: blackberry bushes in gardens, strawberry patches along the sidewalks, and cherry trees lining the roads. We filled our pockets with wild fruit on those long walks, and then we came back with buckets and filled them with berries, eating until our stomachs were bursting, our fingers and faces were purple, and our hearts were overflowing with berry-induced joy.

If raspberries don't happen to be your favorite fruit of the season, don't worry: you can use blueberries or even cherries. Or try mixing berries. Throw in some fresh peaches or apples if you feel like it. Just make it your own. It is summer, after all, and this is the time to be a little wild and free . . . even with recipes. In my experience, if there's fruit baked inside a buttery crust, it's going to be just delightful. Serve this fruity galette with a scoop of ice cream, and you've just about perfectly captured summer in a bowl.

PREP TIME: 40 MINUTES

COOK TIME: 35 TO 40
MINUTES

TOTAL TIME: 80 MINUTES

SERVES: 5 TO 6

FOR THE CRUST

2 teaspoons granulated
sugar

1 teaspoon fine kosher salt

1½ cups all-purpose flour,
plus extra for dusting
work surfaces

¾ cup (1½ sticks) cold
unsalted butter, cut into
small cubes

4 tablespoons ice water,
plus more if necessary

1 large egg yolk, beaten

½ cup sliced almonds

FOR THE FILLING

2 cups fresh raspberries

1 tablespoon freshly
squeezed lemon juice

3 tablespoons firmly
packed brown sugar

1 tablespoon granulated
sugar

½ teaspoon fine kosher salt

Confectioners' sugar for
dusting (optional)

To make the crust, whisk together the sugar, salt, and flour in a medium bowl. Add the butter and toss to coat. Using your fingers or a pastry cutter, blend in the butter until the mixture resembles coarse crumbs.

Turn the mixture out onto a clean work surface and drizzle the ice water over. Using your hands, blend the water into the flour mixture until you can form the dough into a shaggy ball. Add more ice water 1 tablespoon at a time if the mixture is too dry.

Wrap the ball tightly in plastic wrap and chill in the fridge for at least 30 minutes while you make the filling.

In a medium bowl, gently toss together the raspberries, lemon juice, brown sugar, granulated sugar, and salt.

Preheat the oven to 400°F.

Take the dough out of the fridge and roll it out on a lightly floured surface until it forms a roughly 12-inch round. Transfer to a parchment-lined baking sheet.

Add the raspberry filling in the middle of the dough, leaving about a 2-inch border all around.

Fold the edge of the dough partway over the filling, crimping the dough over itself as you go, making sure to leave a large hole open over the fruit. Brush the edges of the crust with the egg yolk and sprinkle the almonds around the crust.

Bake the galette for 35 to 40 minutes, or until the crust is golden brown and the fruit is soft. Allow to cool completely before slicing. Dust with confectioners' sugar if desired.

HITTING THE ROAD

Summer Getaway Essentials

I love road trips. When Marcus and I lived in California, we tried to take road trips as much as we could, especially to see the amazing national parks. I have such fond memories of road-trippin' from LA to San Francisco, Sacramento, Lake Tahoe, Yellowstone, Yosemite, and Joshua Tree. Each trip has its own story, its own share of snafus, squabbles, inside jokes, and special memories that I treasure.

These days, road trips look a little bit different now that we live on the other side of the country and have a baby and two golden retrievers along for the ride. But even though logistics may not be as simple as they used to be, our family is committed to seeking adventure. That said, we never leave home unprepared.

Whether you're hitting the road for a weekend at the lake, a romantic getaway, or an epic cross-country drive, a road trip is a great way to step out of your comfort zone and chase down some adventure. Here are the modern road trip essentials we pack and take with us wherever we go.

FOR MOM AND DAD

- Premade protein-rich snack bags

- Small cooler for fresh fruit and iced coffee

- Two large Nalgene or Stanley water bottles or jugs

- On-the-go first aid kit, including aspirin, sunscreen, face masks, and hand sanitizer

- Reusable insulated travel mugs for water and iced tea

- Two phone charging cables (no arguing over a lone charger)

- Portable wireless charger

- Extra pair or two of sunglasses (our most lost personal item)

- America the Beautiful annual national parks pass (you never know when you're going to drive by a national park)

- Frisbee, because you never know when you might need one

- A screenshot of all the maps we might need, in case we lose a signal along the way

- Easy-to-access swimsuits (you never know!) and a fresh change of clothes just in case

FOR BABY AND DOGS

- All James's favorite snacks and drinks

- Two backup changes of clothes for James

- Blanket for James, no matter what time of year it is, for coziness

- Something to shade the car windows for road-trip naps

- James's favorite relaxing songs and stories downloaded onto a phone

- Ziploc bags of dog food

- Mini duffel bag containing dog toys, leashes, Frisbee, etc.

- Emergency diapers, baby wipes, plastic bags, and pacifiers

REFLECTION

If time and money were not an issue and you could travel anywhere in the world right now, where would you go? Whom would you take with you? What would you do there? Then ask yourself why you answered in the way that you did. What would you hope to discover from this experience?

HOMEMADE CHOCOLATE CHUNK COOKIES
(AND ICE CREAM SANDWICHES)

*What could be better than warm homemade chocolate chip cookies,
you ask? Well, how about two homemade chocolate chip cookies with
vanilla ice cream stuffed in between them? This take on the classic
ice cream sandwich is the perfect treat for a hot summer day.*

From family visits to Disney World to road trips in college to my travels in Europe with Marcus, whenever and wherever I travel during the summertime, one of the first things I want to know is: Where is the best ice cream shop in town? And if that shop also happens to serve freshly baked chocolate chip cookies, even better! Because why have only one summertime sweet treat when you can have two?

But to be honest, I don't believe all chocolate chip cookies are created equal. When I want a chocolate chip cookie, I want perfection. I want crispy edges, a gooey center (but not too gooey!), lots of chocolate, and a complex, nutty, buttery flavor.

So after years of trial and error, borrowing a bit from this recipe and a bit from that recipe, I have now—finally—come up with a recipe that results in this kind of cookie. I really am so proud of the recipe below! It's simple, easy, and everyone who tastes the results absolutely loves them.

So whether you eat them on their own fresh out of the oven or pair them up and freeze them for ice cream sandwiches, these cookies are a true crowd-pleaser. And here's a little tip for you: if you decide to make a batch for ice cream sandwiches, don't forget to set aside one or two warm ones to enjoy while you're hard at work. You deserve it.

PREP TIME: 20 MINUTES,
PLUS 1½ HOURS,
INCLUDING TIME TO CHILL

COOK TIME: 10 MINUTES

TOTAL TIME: 2 HOURS

MAKES 12 TO 15 LARGE
COOKIES, OR ENOUGH
FOR 6 ICE CREAM
SANDWICHES

1 cup (2 sticks) unsalted
butter

3¼ cups all-purpose flour

1¼ teaspoons baking
powder

1 teaspoon baking soda

1 teaspoon fine kosher salt

1½ cups firmly packed
dark brown sugar

½ cup granulated sugar

2 large eggs

2 teaspoons vanilla extract
or paste

2½ cups bittersweet
chocolate chunks, plus
extra for garnish

1 cup chopped unsalted
raw pecans

Flaky sea salt for garnish

1 gallon ice cream
(I prefer vanilla bean)

Preheat the oven to 365°F.

Line a baking sheet with parchment paper or a silicone mat.

Melt the butter in a small saucepan over low heat. Set aside.

In a medium bowl, whisk together the flour, baking powder, baking soda, and kosher salt. Set aside.

Pour the melted butter into a large bowl and whisk in both sugars. Add the eggs one at a time, whisking until combined.

Stir in the vanilla. Then gradually add the dry ingredients to the wet mixture. Stir to combine.

Fold in the chocolate chunks and pecans.

Cover the bowl with plastic wrap and allow the dough to rest in the fridge for 15 to 30 minutes.

Using an ice cream scoop, form the chilled dough into balls and place them 2 inches apart on the prepared baking sheet (the cookies will be about 4 inches across). Place a chocolate chunk on top of each dough ball. Bake for 10 to 12 minutes. When the edges start to get golden, remove the cookies from the oven.

Transfer to a cooling rack and put a pinch of flaky sea salt on each cookie, then allow to cool completely.

If you're making ice cream sandwiches (and why not!), place the cooled cookies in the freezer for 1 hour.

Remove the cookies from the freezer. Place one scoop of ice cream on the bottom of a cookie, then top with a second cookie, forming an ice cream sandwich. Tightly wrap the sandwich in plastic wrap and place it back into the freezer immediately. Repeat until you've formed and frozen six sandwiches.

Let the sandwiches sit in the freezer for at least a couple of hours or overnight, then enjoy!

A SEASON
OF BALANCE

THERE IS MY LIFE BEFORE THE ACCIDENT. And there is my life after.

Before the day Marcus and I were victims of a hit-and-run while riding bikes in our neighborhood in LA, my life was a swirling flurry of activity and work and striving to do more, more, more. Though I kept my home and my appearance and my social media feeds tidy enough, my inner life was definitely off-balance. I rarely knew when or where my work ended and my personal life started: there was too much overlap. Because of this, it felt like my daily life was a never-ending to-do list and I was just trying to keep projects moving forward and everyone happy.

I never scheduled real rest or fun into my routine. I was a servant to the urgent: emails late at night, DMs first thing in the morning, and far too many meetings. You get the picture: I was spread pretty thin. I guess I thought, *Hey, this is what life as a young influencer and entrepreneur is supposed to look like,* and so I had to keep up the pace or everything I'd worked so hard for would fall apart. So I kept on going, kept on doing, kept on running a race with no clear finish line in sight. I guess I thought I would set up some work-life boundaries later on. What's that saying—"I'll sleep when I'm dead"? Well, it took a near-death experience for me to realize just how off-balance my life actually was.

The day of the accident, everything changed in an instant. Just like that, the ceaseless busyness and activity came to a screeching halt. Life moved from one extreme to the other: from motion to stillness, from noise to quiet. I spent the next three months confined to beds, both at home and in hospitals. Suddenly life was on hold while my body healed from the trauma of the accident and from the numerous surgeries that came afterward.

During much of that time, I was basically helpless. For months, I needed serious assistance with almost everything: eating, bathing, dressing, going to the bathroom. Let me tell you, I have never been so humbled in my life. For someone who has always wanted her home, routine, and whole life to be organized just so, this was a nearly unbearable adjustment.

It didn't take long, maybe a week or so, before I realized all those "urgent" things that had seemed so important would have to wait. For now, I had one job to do, and that was to rest. Rest and be still. Rest and be grateful that Marcus and I were still alive. Rest and wait to see what life would look like if and when I could stand up and walk again.

The accident changed us both in profound ways. It's true that we were unlucky to be in the wrong place at the wrong time. But it's also true that we were lucky to have so many of the right people there to save our lives. Needless to say, we are forever grateful to the EMTs, doctors, nurses, and physical therapists who put our broken bodies back together. (We also have a newfound appreciation for our bodies themselves—what a miracle!) We are thankful to our friends and families for the tireless care they showed us. I can't imagine where we would be today if those people hadn't been there to help us.

Happily, we were both able to recover fully. Today, not only can we walk, but we can also run and climb and play and swim and live life much as we did before the accident. Heck, I even grew a baby in this post-accident body! Yet in many ways, the healing is still ongoing. The scars are significant, and we see them every day. We touch them and remember. These scars are reminders of the fragility of life and the gift of today.

In the aftermath of the accident and during the long months of recovery, it became clear to me that I needed to make some serious changes to the way I prioritized and organized my life. After we were finally back on our feet and life got back to

"normal," what I wanted—what I needed—was more balance. I needed a healthy and sustainable pattern of daily life that made time for everything that was important to me: my work with YouTube and Kristin Made, hangouts with family and friends, fun, fitness, and, of course, rest. For the first time, rest and recreation became priorities that I committed to planning for. My quest for better balance started with, and continues to rely on, two key ingredients: clear expectations and positive boundaries.

First, my desire for better balance requires that I understand what I really want. That's the expectations part. And since I belong to a family unit and a business team and a social media community, I need to clarify my priorities for myself first. Only then can I communicate these expectations to others and set healthy boundaries so that everybody can get on the same page.

Here's one practical example of why setting boundaries is important and how it can support a balanced lifestyle: if I regularly spend my evenings responding to emails or answering DMs on Instagram, then it's reasonable that my colleagues will expect me to be available for work-related tasks during the evening. That will become the accepted expectation. Now, of course, there are busy times when I will sometimes have to work in the evenings—that's the nature of owning your own business, after all. But as I strive for a better work-life balance, that should be the exception, not the rule. Evenings are my time for hanging out with Marcus and James, snuggling the dogs, and meeting up with friends and family. Setting a clear boundary around that time helps everyone understand that expectation.

Next, if I truly want to honor the idea that evenings are for rest and recreation, then I need to be fully present wherever I am and fully engaged with whomever I'm spending time with (even if I'm just spending quiet time with myself). This means no sneaking peeks at emails or mindlessly scrolling through Instagram or responding to the pile of DMs I know I need to deal with. No way! If I'm going to be serious about this particular boundary, then I will put away my phone (which is my primary work tool) and allow myself to be "off the clock." I want my hands and eyes free of my work tools so that my heart can focus on other things. Instead of my phone in my hand during the evenings, I want to be holding Marcus's hand. Instead of having my computer on my lap all afternoon, I want to make space for James to sit and play and look Mommy right in the eyes.

The truth is, work will always be there in the background, trying to grab our at-tention and pull us away from the things that really matter. And if it isn't work that's distracting us, it's something else. With our phones and computers and tablets by our sides, it seems harder than ever to "turn off" and just be—be present, be still, and be with other people fully. With technology increasingly becoming central to our daily lives, it seems likely that it will become even harder for humans to find a good balance. Or maybe it just means that each of us needs to set clear expectations and establish firm boundaries so that we don't miss out on the best today has to offer: moments of connection with nature, with friends and family, with a song or story or even just ourselves.

When we know what is truly important to us, we will fight to keep those things front and center in our lives. When our priorities are in balance, we can meet each day, each challenge, each moment with confidence, knowing that we're focusing on the first things first. For me, that's my health (mental and physical), my marriage, my family, my friendships, and my work commitments, and then there's everything else. When this level of balanced prioritizing is happening in my life, I know that it will all be okay.

FLUFFY HOMEMADE PITA BREAD
WITH WHIPPED FETA

*The experience of dipping this freshly baked homemade pita bread
into sweet, creamy, and lemony feta dip is simply divine. Plus,
it's the perfect ready-to-serve appetizer when guests arrive early
or dinner prep is taking longer than expected.*

Finding balance in my life also applies to what I'm eating. You know I have a sweet tooth and love to bake bread, but I try to balance that with healthy smoothies and tasty salads. This pita offers the best of both worlds—it's a fluffy, warm bread that tastes indulgent, but dipping it in hummus or this feta dip gives the bread a bright flavor. Plus, you can serve lots of fresh veggies alongside the dip as well. See? The perfect balance!

PREP TIME: 2½ HOURS,
INCLUDING TIME FOR THE
DOUGH TO RISE

COOK TIME: 16 MINUTES

TOTAL TIME: 2 HOURS
AND 46 MINUTES

SERVES 12

FOR THE BREAD

1 cup warm water
(about 110°F)

1 packet (7 grams or 2¼
teaspoons) active dry yeast

1 tablespoon plus 1
teaspoon granulated sugar

3¾ cups bread flour

1½ teaspoons fine kosher
salt

3 tablespoons tahini

¾ cup plain whole-milk
Greek yogurt

FOR THE DIP

6 ounces feta cheese

3 ounces cream cheese,
at room temperature

3 ounces ricotta cheese

2 tablespoons extra-virgin
olive oil

2 teaspoons finely grated
lemon zest

Salt and pepper to taste

FOR THE TOPPING

1 teaspoon sesame seeds,
toasted

¼ teaspoon chili flakes

¼ teaspoon finely grated
lemon zest

2 teaspoons extra-virgin
olive oil

1 tablespoon honey

→

TO MAKE THE BREAD

In a medium bowl, combine the water, yeast, and 1 teaspoon of the sugar. Let the mixture sit until it's foamy on top, about 5 minutes.

In a large mixing bowl or stand mixer fitted with the paddle attachment, combine the flour, salt, and remaining tablespoon of sugar. Add the yeast mixture, tahini, and yogurt. Mix to combine.

Knead the dough, either in the stand mixer or with your hands on a clean work surface, adding more flour or water as needed, until the dough is soft and slightly sticky. Transfer the dough to a lightly oiled bowl, cover with a damp tea towel or plastic wrap, and allow to rise in a warm place until it's doubled in size, about 2 hours.

Preheat the oven to 500°F. Line two baking sheets with parchment paper.

Turn the dough out onto a clean work surface and divide it into 12 equal-size balls. (You can use a kitchen scale or simply eyeball it.) Cover with a damp tea towel and let rise for an additional 20 minutes.

Roll the balls out into 12 circles that are ¼-inch to ½-inch thick.

Place these circles on the baking sheets, leaving room between them for expansion as they bake.

Bake, one sheet at a time, until the pitas are puffy and lightly browned on top, about 8 minutes, rotating the pan after 5 minutes. Keep a close eye on the pitas so they don't overcook; start checking around the 5-minute mark.

Once the pitas are golden brown and puffed up, transfer them to a wire rack to cool.

TO MAKE THE DIP

Combine the feta, cream cheese, ricotta, olive oil, lemon zest, and salt and pepper in the bowl of a food processor. Process on high until ingredients are well mixed and the dip is smooth and creamy, 2 to 3 minutes. Transfer to a serving bowl or refrigerate if not using immediately.

When ready to serve, top the dip with the sesame seeds, chili flakes, lemon zest, and a drizzle of olive oil and honey.

Serve with the homemade pitas and enjoy!

REFLECTION

Step back for a moment and consider the "big picture" of your life as it is today: your friends and family, your work or studies, the media you consume, how you spend your free time, how you spend your money. Then ask yourself a hard question: Are there areas of your life that are out of balance? If so, what do you need to do to realign them so that you can grow in a healthy way?

BLUE TANSY FACE SERUM

In addition to keeping my bathroom and "get ready" spaces nice and tidy, I'm always in search of ways to make my daily life more balanced. When it comes to beauty products and practices, I want my routines to do more than help me look good; I want these rituals to help me *feel* good as well. This means that when it comes to hair care, skin care, and makeup, it's very important to me to use products that are as "clean" as possible—in other words, products that are, at a minimum, free of toxic ingredients and, whenever possible, made from all-natural and/or certified organic ingredients. I'm literally absorbing these products into my body as they soak into my hair, skin, and lips, so they need to be healthy for me and safe for my home and family.

Luckily, there are an increasing number of clean beauty options available these days, many of which you can find wherever you shop. From all-natural shampoos and deodorants to nontoxic sunscreens and facial masks, many of these clean beauty products are good for people and the planet. When it comes to my makeup, the clean beauty-product swaps that I've made involve my primer, foundation, and powder. And since I prefer making my own products whenever I can, I've also found a way to make a clean face serum at home that I absolutely love: this lavender blue tansy skin serum.

If you've never used a face serum before, it's something I use daily and highly recommend. Basically, a good face serum does two positive things for your skin: (1) it acts as a light moisturizer that can be easily absorbed, and (2) because it's made from all-natural essential oils, it revitalizes your face with refreshing minerals and vitamins. Not only

1 2-ounce amber glass bottle with dropper (the amber glass limits the serum's exposure to UV rays)

Argan oil (this is the base of the serum, also known as the carrier oil)

Frankincense essential oil (helps heal skin imperfections)

Blue tansy essential oil (helps clear congested pores, kill bacteria, and reduce redness)

Lavender essential oil (great for revitalizing dry or irritated skin)

does it use safe, natural ingredients that you can find at your favorite pharmacy or health-food store, it's also super simple and fun to make (and a sweet DIY gift for friends).

INSTRUCTIONS

Fill the glass bottle ¾ full with argan oil. Add 20 drops of the frankincense oil, 5 drops of the blue tansy oil, and 3 drops of the lavender oil.

Shake to combine, and it's ready to use! Store the bottle out of direct sunlight and use within 6 months.

TO USE

Wash and dry your face, then gently massage three to five drops of serum into your chin, cheeks, forehead, and neck in the morning and before bed. Your face should feel refreshingly damp but not wet. For best results, allow the serum to dry fully, then apply an all-natural moisturizer (in the mornings—year-round—I use one with UV protection).

SWEET AND SALTY COCONUT GRANOLA

All summer long, our family is on the go. Especially in August,
we try to soak up as much of the summer as we can . . . before it's gone!
This granola is the perfect grab-and-go snack, whether we're road-tripping
or going for a long walk in the woods.

Granola has always had a kind of "goodness on the go" vibe about it. For as long as I can re-member, granola has been part of fun, busy days: whether I was gulping down quick bowls of it for breakfast before my family drove to the beach or snacking on granola bars in the chair-lift during ski trips with my friends or using it to top a post-workout parfait in LA, granola has been a crunchy companion on many trips and outdoor adventures. A good granola kind of has it all: sweetness and savoriness, fruit and nuts, crunchiness and juiciness—it's all there, and that's why it's so satisfying.

Not long ago, I started making my own granola at home. This way I could control the ratio of oats to nuts and the ratio of fruit to seeds. Plus, I could keep an eye on how much sweetener was going in. In any granola, you need at least a little sweetness, of course, but I don't want a granola that's oversweet. This recipe has a nice balance to it, and we use it for lots of things at our house: as a cereal, as a topping for ice cream and yogurt, and as a snack, which is why we always keep a jar of it in the cupboard. You just never know when you're going to need a little granola on the go.

Of course, if you want to modify or personalize the recipe below, go for it. Substitutions are allowed! Adjust flavors and ratios to taste! Then toss your crunchy mix in a travel tub and head outside for your next adventure.

PREP TIME: 10 MINUTES

COOK TIME: 25 MINUTES

TOTAL TIME: 35 MINUTES

SERVES 6 TO 8

3 tablespoons organic coconut oil

¼ cup all-natural smooth peanut butter

2 tablespoons maple syrup

¼ teaspoon ground cinnamon

3 cups rolled oats

½ cup chopped unsalted raw peanuts

½ cup chopped dried bananas

¼ cup chopped unsweetened coconut flakes

¼ cup chopped unsalted raw walnuts

¼ cup chopped unsalted raw pepitas

1 teaspoon coarse sea salt

3 ounces dark chocolate, cut into chunks

Preheat the oven to 325°F. Line a baking sheet with parchment paper.

Heat the coconut oil in a small saucepan over low heat.

Stir in the peanut butter, maple syrup, and cinnamon, and mix until combined.

Separately, in a large bowl, combine the oats, peanuts, bananas, coconut, walnuts, and pepitas.

Pour the warmed coconut-oil mixture over the oat mixture and stir until the dry ingredients are fully coated.

Spread the granola onto the prepared baking sheet and bake for 25 minutes, stirring halfway, or until lightly browned.

Remove the baking sheet from the oven and sprinkle with sea salt.

Allow to rest for 3 to 5 minutes before stirring in the chocolate chunks.

Cool fully on the baking sheet, then store in a large glass jar.

A SEASON FOR MEMORY MAKING

AM I A NOSTALGIC, SENTIMENTAL PERSON? Yes, I would say that I am—to a point. But while I sometimes indulge in walks down memory lane, I know for a fact that I'm not as nostalgic as some people, including my friend Shannon.

Shannon is, hands down, the sweetest person I have ever met. She is also deeply, deeply nostalgic, especially about gifts she has received. Once, when we were roommates in college, I was deep cleaning the bathroom we shared during one of my seasonal purges (oh, yeah, the purges go way back), and while doing so, I found a bottle of Bath & Body Works lotion that I didn't recognize. It was clearly old, like maybe from 1998 . . . maybe 1988! The scent was something like wild rosemary–infused strawberry margarita . . . it wasn't great, trust me. Anyway, it was old, and it needed to go. So I tossed it in the trash. Suddenly, from out of nowhere, Shannon swooped into the bathroom and rescued the old bottle from the garbage. Shocked at my audacity, she told me I absolutely could not throw out the lotion, explaining that it was really special to her.

"Wait—what? Why?" I asked, both surprised and intrigued.

"Because," she said, "it was a gift from one of my favorite teachers in middle school."

Shannon was 100 percent serious. More serious than I had ever seen her before. She was not going to let me throw away this weird old lotion.

"Wait, Shannon," I protested. "A gift from middle school—*middle school*?" I was flabbergasted. I tried to appeal to her practical side. "I'm sure it's expired by now, right? We should probably throw it out."

Shannon seemed astonished by my monstrous, coldhearted suggestion to dispose of the lotion. "It doesn't matter. It was a gift, so you cannot throw it away. It stays."

And that was that: end of conversation. I gave up, and that ancient lotion stayed in our bathroom for the following year. For all I know, Shannon still has it today.

I learned something about my roommate that day, and I made a point from then on to only give her super-thoughtful, long-lasting gifts. But the incident made me question myself as well. Was I too nonchalant about the gifts I received? Was I not thankful enough? Was I really a coldhearted, purge-loving monster?

Finally, I decided that we all exist at different places on the sentimentality spectrum. While Shannon treats every gift she receives as a true treasure imbued with meaning and value, I want my life and spaces to be as serene as possible, which requires vigilant defense against the armies of clutter that tirelessly try to infiltrate my life. It's just two different ways of looking at our relationship to stuff. Neither is necessarily better than the other; they're just different. I guess you could say one woman's trash is another woman's prized bottle of teacher-gifted rosemary margarita hand lotion. And that's okay.

I've never been one to hang on to material things just because they were gifts or because I might—maybe, perhaps, just in case—someday need them. Yes, I do believe that some objects are truly special and should be kept, maybe even passed on someday to my kids, but these kinds of objects are rare and have to have some meaningful association to a person, place, or event. I have a few one-of-a-kind keepsakes that have come down to me from my parents and grandparents, little mementos that I treasure. Each of these keepsakes originates in someone else's life, and some even come from faraway places, and yet now they are in my care for a little while.

While certain objects can help light the candle of memory, for me, it's thinking back to shared meaningful experiences that will inevitably awaken a bonfire of emotion and nostalgia. My collected memories—like yours, I assume—are a kind of collage of the best and worst of my life. If I made a list of my all-time favorite memories—

those moments that truly define me as an individual—the list would span from my earliest childhood (Christmas morning! Learning to ski! Learning to ride my bike! The family dogs!) up through the days when James took his first steps and said his first words. It makes me smile just to think of this list—a kind of greatest-hits compilation of my first three decades.

These memories help anchor me in the context of the world and remind me where I've come from, what I've done, and how I've changed. These days, I also recognize that I have the opportunity to shape not only my own future memories, but also the first memories of my children. This is a privilege that Marcus and I do not take lightly. We are committed to trying to create a lifetime of great memories for our kids and for each other. A big part of why we fell in love and got married was because we have a shared belief that, by and large, life will be what you make of it. But we know that memory making rarely happens passively. Sure, spontaneity can occasionally provide amazing memory-making opportunities. But that doesn't mean we're going to sit around and wait for the stars to align in order to create new memories. No way!

We want to be active memory makers, filling our emotional storehouses with new, fun, and interesting experiences whenever we can in order to strengthen both our friendship and our marriage. Ever since

James was born, we have tried to do this in two ways.

First, we try to make at least one new memory every week. This can be eating at a new restaurant, going for a hike on a new trail, or taking a day trip to a town we've never been to before. Simple stuff; nothing huge.

Second, we aim to take a trip out of state at least three or four times per year as a family. This might just be for a day or two, or for a weekend, or for a proper weeklong vacation. But the point is, we either go to places we haven't been before (explore and discover!) or revisit a place we know we love (rediscover and reconnect!). Doing this helps satisfy two big needs in our relationship: to always have something to look forward to and plan together, and to actively and regularly make new memories together.

Not every new memory is a keeper. In fact, we've already forgotten a lot of the things we tried and did. But the ones that stick, stick hard! And those are the memories we treasure and can't wait to share with James. These are the things that pop up in conversation when we're just driving around or sitting on the sofa. "Remember when we . . ." is a phrase that will almost always bring a smile to our faces. This has

been so fun and life-giving for us. It also helps us weather difficulties and struggles. When we argue or disagree or just get busy and feel disconnected, these memories bring us back to each other. Our shared memories are a red thread in our lives that bind us together and make us stronger.

In the long term, we hope this investment in memory making will help keep our relationship vibrant and instill a love for adventure, risk taking, and discovery in our kids. Marcus and I agree: if we can invest in lots of great memories now, while we're young, healthy, and active, then we will surely grow old and happy together. Someday we'll just be two old coots sitting in our rocking chairs, talking about all the fun, outlandish things we did. The grandkids will think we're strange, I'm sure—just another pair of super-sentimental seniors telling their stories about the old days, stories that get told over and over again. Well, they get told over and over again because they are the souvenirs of a life well lived.

Whatever season of life you are in right now, it's the perfect time to invest in making meaningful memories—with your partner, your friends, your kids, your parents, and even just yourself. It's good for the body and soul, and I believe you will reap the benefits for many years to come.

AT-HOME PIZZA NIGHT WITH FRIENDS

A casual homemade-pizza night is the perfect way
to gather good friends around good food.

One of Marcus's and my favorite weekend traditions is to have a bunch of friends over for pizza night. I provide the premade homemade dough and ask guests to potluck the toppings and drinks. Then we gather around and build a variety of pizzas.

I bake as many at once as I can, but it happens in shifts, so we eat each one as it comes out, and we all get to try one another's creations a slice at a time. It's a fun and easy way to make a dinner party both interactive and spontaneous. The pizzas are never exactly the same—certainly never boring—but they are always delicious!

Below is my super-easy recipe for homemade pizza dough alongside three of my all-time favorite tried-and-true topping recipes. Of course, the beauty of pizza is that there is almost no way to mess it up (the jury is still out on pineapple, though).

Mix it up, experiment, collaborate, and have fun. Who knows? Maybe you will come up with the next great innovation in pizza!

PREP TIME: 80 MINUTES,
INCLUDING TIME FOR
THE DOUGH TO RISE

COOK TIME: 15 MINUTES

TOTAL TIME: 95 MINUTES

SERVES 4

---

1 packet (7 grams, or 2¼ teaspoons) active dry yeast

1 cup warm water (about 110°F)

1 teaspoon granulated sugar

PIZZA DOUGH

Combine the yeast, water, and sugar in a large mixing bowl and let it sit for 5 minutes, or until the mixture foams and bubbles at the surface.

Add the salt and flour and combine with a spoon until a dough begins to form.

Transfer to a lightly floured surface and knead until smooth.

Lightly coat a large mixing bowl with the olive oil. Transfer the dough to the bowl, cover with plastic wrap, and let it rest somewhere warm (my favorite place is in the oven with the heat turned off but the light turned on).

⟶

½ teaspoon fine kosher salt

2½ cups all-purpose flour, plus extra for dusting the work surface

Olive oil for greasing

Let the dough rise for 30 to 60 minutes, or until it has doubled in size.

Preheat the oven to 500°F. If you're using a pizza stone, allow it to preheat at the same time as the oven.

Transfer the risen dough to a floured surface and gently knead it until smooth.

Roll out the dough into a circle approximately 12 inches in diameter.

Using your thumb, indent a circle about 1 inch from the edge of the dough. This will form the outer crust.

Top with your favorite sauce and toppings.

Transfer the pizza to a baking sheet or pizza stone and bake for 12 to 15 minutes, or until the crust is golden brown.

CLASSIC PIZZA MARGHERITA

1 to 2 tablespoons extra-virgin olive oil

1 recipe Pizza Dough (page 151)

½ cup homemade tomato sauce

½ cup fresh mozzarella, sliced

Generous pinch of sea salt

Handful of fresh basil leaves

Shredded Parmesan cheese to taste

This simple pizza is legendary for a reason. Go to any pizzeria in Italy, and you'll find this on the menu. Made with simple, wholesome ingredients, the classic margherita pizza is like pizza 1.0—easy as pie to make yourself but always so good. It's a good foundational recipe that you can easily change up with different toppings. I've also included two of my favorite variations.

Preheat the oven to 500°F. If you're using a pizza stone, allow it to preheat at the same time as the oven.

Brush the olive oil evenly over your unbaked pizza dough. You want the dough shiny but not soggy.

Gently spread the tomato sauce evenly over the crust with the back of a spoon.

Top with the mozzarella.

Dust the whole pie with sea salt. Bake for 12 to 15 minutes, then top with fresh basil leaves and Parmesan cheese and enjoy.

VARIATIONS

Prosciutto, Fig, and Ricotta: Skip the tomato sauce and brush 1 to 2 tablespoons of olive oil over the crust. Top with half a cup of fresh sliced mozzarella, a few dollops of ricotta, and six ounces of prosciutto. Bake for 12 to 15 minutes. Let cool for a few minutes, then add two quartered figs, a handful of arugula, salt and pepper, and a tablespoon of hot honey (or to taste). Garnish with Parmesan cheese and enjoy.

Crowd Pleaser for Meat Lovers: Follow the same steps as for the pizza margherita, but after adding the sauce, top your crust with sliced pepperoni, chopped pancetta, and fully cooked ground hot Italian sausage. The meat should cover the top of the crust. Add half a cup of fresh mozzarella, sliced, around the top of the meat. Bake for 12 to 15 minutes, then garnish with Parmesan cheese and red pepper flakes to taste.

CAPTURED MEMORIES

The Timeless Art
of Pressing Wildflowers

I'm a sucker for all kinds of flowers: bouquets from the florist, spring wildflowers picked from the side of the road, decorative dried flowers, and especially, pressed wildflowers. There's something really lovely about an individual flower preserved and displayed as an important specimen of natural beauty. This simple guide is an easy introduction to a craft that brings together the beauty of nature and your own creativity in order to make a memory of summer—a treasure whose life and color have been carefully preserved to encourage and inspire you throughout the seasons of the year.

BEFORE YOU START

Research the kinds of wildflowers that grow in your area. Once you know which ones you like best, you will know what to look for. Then watch the calendar and wait for the time when these flowers are in bloom. Keep an eye out when walking, driving, or biking around. Tip: the fresher the flowers, the better your pressings will be.

- The leaves of trees, shrubs, and herbs can also be pressed. Try collecting leaves and flowers with complementary colors and textures, then arranging them together once all have been pressed.

- As a rule of thumb, the easiest flowers to press are those with just a single layer of petals and flat heads, such as buttercups, violets, blue columbine, wild flax, jasmine, and prairie stars. These will be

WHAT YOU'LL NEED

Wildflowers of your choice

Several heavy books

Parchment paper or tissue paper (not paper towels)

the best at retaining their color and shape and will take the least amount of time to dry.

INSTRUCTIONS

Collect wildflowers while they are in bloom. Take care to pick the stems and a few leaves along with the flowers you've chosen. This will both help the flower preserve its shape and color and will look nice in the frame after pressing. Try to avoid flowers with petal damage or blemishes.

1. Make sure the wildflowers are completely dry. Separate the leaves from the stems. Using the inside of a heavy book as your work surface, carefully arrange the flowers and leaves on one half of a piece of parchment paper. Leave room between flowers so there is no overlap.

2. Carefully fold the parchment over the flowers and leaves so they are completely covered. Close the book gently. Don't worry: the parchment paper will protect the pages from damage and discoloration.

3. Place a heavy object on top of the book and wait. Every flower is different: some take more time than others, especially if the flowers are thick or have a big head. I typically wait three to four weeks before removing the flowers from the book. But honestly, I sometimes forget where I've tucked away my little pressings, and then later, when I open or move the book, I get a lovely surprise!

4. When you can't wait any longer, carefully open the book and use tweezers or tongs to transfer the pressed flowers to a flat surface. Be gentle: pressed flowers are fragile, delicate little beauties. Treat them with extra care.

TIPS

There are a lot of ways to display your lovely pressed flowers. Personally, I love the simplicity of a wooden picture frame . . .

Hang on the wall, place on a shelf, or wrap and give as a gift. Then enjoy your beautifully unique, custom-pressed wildflower artwork.

MOVIE-NIGHT CARAMEL CORN

*Whether it's just for you, for you and a friend, or for a house
full of guests, this super-easy recipe puts an especially
sweet spin on everybody's favorite movie-night snack: popcorn.*

I love a cozy movie night! Comedy, action, adventure, mystery—it doesn't really matter to me as long as it's not too scary and there are plenty of soft blankets, a dog or two to snuggle with, and lots of snacks. A movie night is also a fun way to connect with others and make memories. If the vibe is good and the movie is fun, you might even end up having a super-memorable time together. But of course, no matter if it's a movie night for two or twenty-two, you gotta have popcorn!

With caramel corn you get it all—salty and sweet, crunchy and creamy, airy and indulgent. Plus, you can always customize and make your own perfect version of this caramel corn. Just mix in whatever nuts, chocolate morsels, or dried fruits you love and make this treat your very own.

Also, consider setting up a snack station in the kitchen or on a sideboard near the screen. Along with your yummy homemade caramel corn, you can set out bowls of various fruits, nuts, and little chocolate treats. That way you (as the host) don't have to be so back-and-forth and instead can just settle in and enjoy while others make their own snack plates just before the lights go dim and the movie comes to life.

PREP TIME: 5 MINUTES

COOK TIME: 10 MINUTES

TOTAL TIME: 15 MINUTES

SERVES 4 TO 6

½ cup popcorn kernels

1 cup (2 sticks) unsalted butter

1 cup granulated sugar

1 teaspoon vanilla extract

3 tablespoons water

Generous pinch of fine kosher salt

Unsalted nuts, chopped dried fruit, chocolate chips, and/or sea salt (optional)

Pop popcorn according to package directions and set aside to cool. Lay a piece of parchment paper on the counter to create a work surface.

To make the caramel, in a small saucepan over medium heat, combine the butter, sugar, vanilla, water, and salt. Heat, stirring constantly, until all ingredients are melted and start to bubble. When the mixture reaches about 290°F to 300°F on a candy thermometer and turns a nice nutty-brown color, remove from the heat.

Evenly spread the cooled popcorn in a heat-safe baking dish. Pour the hot liquid caramel over the popcorn and stir. Be careful to distribute the caramel evenly so that it coats each individual piece of popcorn.

Spoon the popcorn mixture onto the parchment paper and spread it out. Allow to cool fully, about 10 minutes.

Transfer the popcorn to a large serving bowl, and crunch it up, breaking apart the large chunks with your hands for easier snacking later on.

Optional: For an even sweeter, saltier, or crunchier caramel corn, you can mix in nuts, dried fruit, chocolate chips, or a pinch of sea salt.

REFLECTION

Have you ever made a list of your fondest memories? If not, I encourage you to try: it's a fun and meaningful exercise. Just take out a pen and start jotting down your favorite moments from childhood up until today. Don't overthink it; just make quick notes. When you're done, consider adding a second column to your list—future memories you want to make. Include the names of the people you want to share these future memories with. Then share these ideas with those closest to you and get busy making new memories!

A SEASON
TO HARVEST

A PERFECT AUTUMN DAY GOES SOMETHING like this . . .

You wake up slow with nowhere to go. When you finally pull yourself out from under a mountain of cozy comforters, it's time for a cup of coffee—or five—so you start your day off with a honey-and-cinnamon latte, because why not? After breakfast, the sun beckons you to come outside, so you bundle up and go for a walk. On days like these, you can feel the sun on your face and the wind in your hair as you watch your breath rise like woodsmoke into the crisp October air. When you get back, maybe there will be a warm, crumbly dessert to munch on, and maybe some spiced cider or mulled wine, while you listen to the wind pull the last of the leaves down from the trees.

For most of my life, I've lived in Florida and California, places where there aren't typically four distinct seasons each year. But now that we're living in Tennessee, we actually experience four unique seasons, each with its own character and beauty. There's part of me that wishes it could always be fall, which is unquestionably the coziest time of year.

At its core, fall is a season of dramatic change in the natural world. It's a precursor of things to come, and each year, this change affects me deeply, in both my body and my mind. During the fall, I can feel a soft melancholy come upon me. It's not sadness, exactly, but a new depth of thoughtfulness, like nostalgia mixed with gratitude and uncertainty about things to come. Autumn is such a magical and mysterious season, rich with the promise of change.

In truth, these days I sometimes find myself actively avoiding change so that I don't have to deal with conflict, either between myself and others or just within myself. Change can be really hard, because we don't know what the future holds or whether we'll ever go back to the way things were. Even if the way things were wasn't great, at least it was familiar. But change can also lead us into something new and exciting.

In my experience, the outward changes in life are usually the most dramatic (and often the scariest!). We move to a new town; we start a new job; we end a long-term relationship—these events happen first and are followed by inner changes that can take weeks, months, or even years to understand and accept. Sometimes seasons pass by and we find that we're still struggling to settle into a new normal.

When I've gone through seasons like this, regrets about the past and fears about the future battle to distract me from where I am right now. Over the past few years, I've gone through several of these big life shifts: I relocated from California to Tennessee; I went from being single to being married; I transitioned from life before our big accident to life after; I went from being pregnant to being a full-time mom. See what I mean? The only constant is change! There's only one thing we can do: learn how to find something worth appreciating in every season, no matter where we are in the calendar year or in our own personal journey.

What we call fall used to be called harvest season by many people and cultures. Even today, fall is often when urbanites and suburbanites (like me) can feel most connected to local farms and farmers. This is when we go for hayrides and visit pumpkin patches, and pick apples and learn how to make preserves. Traditionally, harvest has always been a time when the last of the produce grown during the spring and summer is brought in from the fields. Farmers enjoy the fruits of their hard work, and fresh foods are preserved for the long winter ahead. Traditional harvest-season activities can be such a beautiful blend of gratitude for past bounty and hope for future sustenance.

Whatever season we are in right now, it won't last forever. Colors are going to fade. Cold winds are going to blow. Daylight is going to dim. But despite all that, even the winter won't last forever; it's only a season. And each season is worth celebrating, if only we can remember to be thankful for the many gifts we've received on the journey so far and if we can remember to be hopeful even in the darkest days of winter.

Thinking of the fall as a season of harvest helps me do this. It helps me enjoy the transition and embrace the change. It helps me be grateful for all I have experienced in the spring and summer. It helps me look ahead in anticipation of more good gifts, future challenges, and lessons learned, and it helps me remember that there are more green fields and warm days ahead. Spring will be here soon, autumn reminds me. Soon, yes, but not just yet. For now, I'll enjoy the cozy knits and apple crumble.

ONE-PAN CRISPY HERB-ROASTED CHICKEN

This is my favorite home-cooked meal when I want to serve a simple but special dinner that will make guests feel welcome and appreciated. The secret here is the fragrant herbs that make this rustic dish a timeless classic.

Honestly, roast chicken and veggies is one of the easiest meals to make. It's warm and comforting, hearty and flavorful. But a roast chicken can be a bit bland if you skimp on the special details. Luckily, the special details in this recipe could not be simpler—the delightful culinary triple threat of fresh herbs, cracked black pepper, and bright, zesty lemon. Trust me: when you introduce these ingredients, your family, your guests, and your taste buds will definitely notice the difference. Your roast chicken dinners will never be the same.

PREP TIME: 20 MINUTES

COOK TIME: 1½ HOURS

TOTAL TIME: 2 HOURS

SERVES 4 TO 6

1 whole chicken, with skin on (5 to 7 pounds)

3 tablespoons butter, at room temperature

Fine kosher salt to taste

Cracked black pepper to taste

Several sprigs fresh thyme

Several sprigs fresh rosemary

1 lemon, halved

1 head garlic, outer skin removed and halved crosswise

1 large white onion, peeled and cut into quarters

½ pound fingerling or new potatoes

3 to 5 large carrots, peeled and cut into 2-inch segments

2 tablespoons extra-virgin olive oil

$\longrightarrow$

Preheat the oven to 400°F.

Remove any giblets from the chicken and discard them or save for another use. Using your fingers or a pastry brush, spread the butter over the outside of the chicken and under the skin.

Liberally season the chicken with salt and pepper.

Stuff the cavity of the chicken with the thyme, rosemary, lemon halves, and garlic.

Place the onion, potatoes, and carrots in the bottom of a roasting pan. Drizzle with the olive oil, season with salt and pepper, and toss until coated. Spread the veggies evenly across the bottom of the pan and place the chicken on top.

Roast the chicken for 60 to 90 minutes. To test for doneness, place a meat thermometer in the thickest part of the thigh without touching the bone. If it registers between 165°F and 175°F, then it's ready.

Remove the roasting pan from the oven and cover with foil. Allow the chicken to rest for 20 minutes before carving and serving alongside the potatoes, onions, and carrots from the roasting pan.

THE SOFT GLOW
OF CANDLELIGHT

Making Your Own
All-Natural Beeswax Candles

Honeybees are amazing—they really are! They can live almost any-where. They pollinate our trees and flowers; they're social; they're mas-ter builders; they produce honey; their hives are run by powerful queens. On top of all that, they produce beeswax, a natural product that has almost unlimited domestic applications. You can use it to make natural soaps, lotions, crayons, lip balms, wood conditioners, a waterproofing cream for clothes and shoes, and, of course, nontoxic candles.

Back when I learned that store-bought paraffin candles release car-cinogens as they burn, I knew it was time to make a change. When I started researching alternatives, I learned about the ancient art of making candles from beeswax, and I just had to try it. On the follow-ing pages I outline the simple step-by-step process I use and offer a few tips and tricks to help you begin.

Once you start working with beeswax, I think you'll be amazed at how versatile it is. Along with being entirely natural and safe to use, it has a delightfully subtle honey-hinted scent that I have come to love around our house.

WHAT YOU'LL NEED

Recyclable metal coffee can

Large pot big enough to contain the coffee can without crowding

1 pound natural beeswax, either in sheets or pellets (pellets break down more easily)

Disposable stirrer

½ cup organic coconut oil

50 drops essential oil of your choice (optional)

Natural candle wicks, one for each candle

6 4-ounce mason jars or 3 half-pint mason jars (you can also make these as tapers, but I find this to be the easiest place to start)

Wick stickers (one for each candle), hot glue, or double-sided tape

Bamboo skewers or chopsticks, one for each candle

INSTRUCTIONS

1. Place the coffee can inside the large pot and fill the large pot with water until it comes halfway up the sides of the can. Bring the water to a simmer over medium heat.

2. Place the beeswax in the coffee can and stir frequently until the beeswax is melted and fully liquefied. It can be helpful to use a disposable stirrer like a wooden chopstick, since it will be hard to clean the beeswax off after. Be careful not to splash water into the melted wax.

3. Turn off the heat, remove the coffee can from the pot, and stir in the coconut oil.

4. If you want a scented beeswax candle, now is the time to add the essential oils of your choice. But don't add them too early, or they will evaporate. Allow the wax to harden slightly before adding the oils. I like the natural, subtle honey scent of the beeswax itself. But it's worth experimenting with essential oils if you want to customize the scent to your liking.

5. Affix a wick to the inside bottom of a mason jar. You can do this a number of ways, with a drop of hot glue or double-sided tape or store-bought wick stickers. I typically use the wick stickers for ease. Make sure the wick is centered. Repeat with the other wicks and mason jars.

6. Lay a skewer or chopstick across the top of each jar and wrap the excess wick around it. This will keep the wick standing straight up and centered while the wax hardens.

7. Pour the wax mixture evenly into the jars, leaving about an inch of space at the top.

⟶

8. Allow the wax to harden completely overnight.

9. Once the wax has hardened, trim the wicks to about a ½ inch. Your candles are now ready to use. Bonus: when your beeswax candles are nearly all used up, you can replace the wick stickers and reuse the jars for another batch of candles.

TIPS

Always handle fire, flames, and candles with extreme care.

Beeswax can burn very hot, so it's a good idea to place your homemade candles on a nonflammable surface such as ceramic, stone, or marble and not directly onto wood or other sensitive materials.

Liquid and melted wax can be very hard to clean off your appliances, utensils, and dishes.

Note that because beeswax candles are slow to burn, they require thicker, sturdier wicks than what's used for paraffin candles.

Get creative and use old coffee mugs or vintage containers to hold the wax. Anything that is heat-resistant can make a cute candleholder.

HEARTY LENTIL SOUP

Paired with a slice of fresh sourdough bread, this hearty soup has the power to warm the body and the soul on a chilly evening. Nourishing and easy to make, this is one of my go-to meals once autumn arrives.

There aren't that many foods that I regularly crave. But one exception is homemade soup, which I really love during the fall or anytime I'm feeling under the weather. In particular, I often get a craving for this veggie-rich lentil soup, which absolutely never fails to comfort me. Since lentils are high in protein, this soup tastes richer, heartier, and more filling than most brothy soups. Of course, the rich texture also makes it perfect as a dip for fresh sourdough bread or even a crispy grilled cheese sandwich.

PREP TIME: 10 MINUTES

COOK TIME: 25 MINUTES

TOTAL TIME: 35 MINUTES

SERVES 6 TO 8

1 tablespoon extra-virgin olive oil

1 medium yellow onion, diced

4 medium carrots, diced

1 cup diced celery (about 3 stalks)

5 cups chicken broth

1 15-ounce can crushed tomatoes, drained

1 teaspoon fine kosher salt

1 teaspoon black pepper

2 teaspoons onion powder

2 teaspoons garlic powder

1 tablespoon chicken bouillon powder (optional)

2 cups uncooked jasmine rice

2 cups cooked lentils (any type will do)

1 cup baby spinach leaves

Fresh parsley leaves for garnish

→

In a large pot, heat the olive oil over medium heat. Add the onion, carrots, and celery, and sauté until the onions are translucent and all the veggies are tender.

Add the chicken broth, tomatoes, salt, pepper, onion powder, garlic powder, and bouillon, if desired.

Simmer over medium heat for 20 minutes.

Meanwhile, prepare the rice according to package directions.

Add the cooked lentils and spinach to the soup and simmer for about 2 minutes, or until the spinach is wilted.

Season to taste and serve over cooked rice. Garnish each bowl with parsley.

REFLECTION

What types of gatherings do you like to host? Small, intimate dinner parties with a couple of friends? Big, loud outdoor barbecues with the neighbors? Consider how you can use gatherings (whether big or small) to make meaningful, life-affirming connections with others, then lean in to what feels most life-giving and plan a gathering this month.

A SEASON
FOR GRATITUDE

I KNOW IT'S ALWAYS THE BIGGEST CHALLENGES in life that lead to the most meaningful seasons of personal growth, and the last few years for me have been an endless cycle of new challenges. But dang—it's never easy, is it?

As I look back, I recall one period of time that was especially overwhelming. The short version goes like this: in the course of a single year, we had our accident (see August) and spent months in serious physical pain trying to recover. Then we went through the process of moving to Tennessee without knowing where we were going to settle (see March), living out of suitcases for months while I was pregnant and the whole world was fighting a pandemic. Then came James's birth, a time of joy intermingled with months of postpartum blues. During that long year, it felt like life would never be uncomplicated again.

Okay, now it's time for some real talk: I don't like to admit it, but during that year, I must have been difficult to be around. I was irritable. I complained. I was easily annoyed and short-tempered. I had lost all sense of spontaneity and felt joyless. Marcus might not ever admit it, but I'm sure that during that season of life, living with me was pretty unbearable at times. If you asked, I proba-bly couldn't have told you exactly what was bothering me. In fact, I probably would have told you that I was fine. But the truth is, something big was going on in my heart. In the midst of the changes and challenges, I had lost something that was essential to who I am, something that keeps me moving forward—joy.

I have always been a pretty sunny, optimistic, and hopeful person. I have lots of people to love and who love me. I have been privileged in so many ways, and I have a great life, despite this season of struggles. But somewhere along the way, sadness had crept in, maybe through a side door, maybe while I was stuck in hospital beds, or maybe it was when I watched my pregnant body change and expand until I was unrecognizable to myself. Maybe it was the combination of all these things.

But it was more than that. I had lost the *root* of joy, which is always gratitude. Without joy rooted in gratitude, I couldn't experience my relationships and my life as a blessing and inspiration. Everything suffered as a result: my health, my marriage, my work, my friendships. It was a dark time for me, and honestly, it's not easy to write about it here. But it happened.

One day I stumbled across a sermon in

which the pastor said, "The root of joy is found in gratitude." It was just a single phrase, an aside to his teaching, but those words helped me snap out of my emotional funk and reset my outlook after the long year of challenges. I don't want to minimize any pain, hurt, or struggles you might be experiencing in your own challenging season, and I believe in taking advantage of all sorts of help—including talking with loved ones or a therapist. But in my case, I started to pray for a renewed sense of joy in my life, for a heart filled with genuine gratitude, and for a greater appreciation for the gift of the people around me. And this is still my prayer today. I truly believe that my joy grows directly in proportion to my sense of gratitude.

From that moment, I made two commitments to myself: first, to be consciously grateful every day and at various times throughout the day. Second, to try to focus less on myself and more on others.

These days, as soon as I wake up—before I glance at my phone or climb out of bed— I ask myself, "What am I thankful for today?" If the sun is peeking through the windows, I think, *Wow, a sunny day!* If James slept through the night, I think, *I'm so grateful to feel well-rested!* Some days this practice of gratitude runs in the background, and other days, I need to speak my gratitude out loud, literally talk

to myself and say, "Even though it's hard [or inconvenient or messy or annoying], I'm thankful for this challenge." I will also write sticky notes with just two words on them—*be thankful*—and hide them in various places (in drawers, in the car, in my wallet) so I can encounter them throughout the day. I find that this visual reminder reinforces my ability to make gratitude a daily practice.

The second part of my new lifestyle of gratitude is all about focusing on other people. When I was reaching an emotional breaking point during that stressful year, something occurred to me: most of my thoughts were hung up on the things that *I* felt were missing or were challenging in *my* life. Looking back, I can see now that the result of all of this me-centered thinking was that I was unable to be grateful for all the good things I had and that joy was nearly impossible to experience or share with others. But as soon as I started to pivot my thoughts toward other people, I could immediately feel a positive shift. Expressing gratitude for these people allowed my joy to return.

When I was consciously thankful for a loving husband and a healthy baby boy, it eased my postpartum struggles. Recognizing that we have friends—both old and new—around us in Nashville smoothed the transition process after we moved. Having sisters who were willing to just be there and listen and tell me I was going to be fine was a powerful force in helping me come out of my funk.

Then there was the whole online community of women who shared insights and stories about becoming a mom, running a business, or just getting through rough days. These women took time out of their busy lives to send me encouraging messages, and when I felt grateful to each of them, every DM, email, and Instagram comment became a little seed of joy in my life.

Where is there room for more gratitude in your life? Are there new and greater blessings that await you? Are there new and greater blessings that await all of us if we just remember to look up and around at the natural world, our families and communities, and the gifts of sight and sound and touch and taste and be grateful? I am certain there are. I hope we can grow together in gratitude this season and see what joys lie just around the corner.

REFLECTION

I know it sounds a bit cheesy, but gratitude really is an attitude. When I'm having a hard day, sometimes the most helpful thing is to focus on something I'm thankful for, even something small. What are one or two things you're thankful for today? Try to let your gratitude for these blessings overflow into the rest of your mindset.

FESTIVE FALL POTPIE

*Thanksgiving celebrations are all about the three Fs: family,
friends, and, of course, food! But there's no reason why our
Thanksgiving meals can't include variations on classic dishes.
This festive fall potpie is a twist on a classic Turkey Day tradition.*

This season is all about keeping gratitude at the forefront of our minds, and if there's one thing I'm always thankful for, it's traditional Thanksgiving foods. For several years, I've been on a mission to discover, adapt, innovate, and create Turkey Day–adjacent variants that uphold the spirit of traditional Thanksgiving gatherings but also keep things interesting. Along the way, some things have worked (fresh-baked cranberry bread and homemade apple pie milkshakes were both a hit!), while others have failed (grilled turkey burgers with cornbread buns—yikes!). But it certainly makes cooking for the season more fun and inspiring for me.

These savory potpies are certainly in the spirit of Thanksgiving, but they bring something refreshing to any gathering (plus, they freeze and travel very easily).

PREP TIME: 1½ HOURS,
INCLUDING TIME FOR
THE DOUGH TO CHILL

COOK TIME: 30 TO 40
MINUTES

TOTAL TIME: 2 HOURS
AND 10 MINUTES

SERVES 6

FOR THE CRUST

2½ cups all-purpose flour

1 teaspoon fine sea salt

1 cup (2 sticks) very cold
unsalted butter, cut into
½-inch cubes

8 to 12 tablespoons
ice water

FOR THE FILLING

4 tablespoons butter

1 cup finely diced
yellow onion

1 cup finely diced celery

1 cup finely diced carrots

Salt and pepper to taste

3 cloves garlic, minced

1 teaspoon onion powder

1 teaspoon fresh thyme
leaves

1 teaspoon fresh
rosemary leaves

⅓ cup all-purpose flour

2 cups chicken broth

½ cup heavy cream

1 teaspoon chicken
bouillon powder

→

2 cups cooked shredded turkey breast or boneless, skinless chicken breast

1 cup peeled and diced cooked yellow potatoes

½ cup frozen peas

1 cup frozen corn

1 large egg, beaten

Fresh sprigs of thyme and rosemary for garnish

TO MAKE THE CRUST

Combine the flour and salt in a large bowl and mix well.

Using a pastry cutter or your fingers, mix in the butter until the mixture forms pea-size clumps.

Add the ice water, a few tablespoons at a time, stirring gently with a wooden spoon until the dough comes together but is still crumbly. The dough is ready when it holds its shape if you squeeze some of it in your hands.

Gather the dough together and separate it into two equal-size balls. These will be your bottom and top crusts.

Gently wrap the dough balls in plastic wrap and refrigerate for 1 hour.

Remove one dough ball from the fridge and allow it to sit at room temperature for a few minutes to soften.

Roll out the softened dough ball into a circle that is slightly larger than a pie plate. Gently press the dough into the pie plate.

Set the pie plate in the fridge.

TO MAKE THE FILLING

Melt the butter in a 12-inch skillet over medium heat. Sauté the onions, celery, and carrots until tender, about 4 to 5 minutes. Add salt and pepper. Add the garlic, onion powder, thyme, and rosemary. Toss to coat and cook for 1 to 2 more minutes.

Add the flour and stir. Cook for about 2 minutes.

→

Gradually stir in the chicken broth, stirring until fully combined. Adding the liquid too quickly will break the roux and interfere with the thickness of the gravy.

Gradually stir in the heavy cream.

Add the bouillon then the shredded meat, and stir to combine.

Add the potatoes, peas, and corn. Stir until heated through.

Remove from the heat and allow to partially cool for 1 to 2 minutes.

TO MAKE THE PIE

Preheat the oven to 425°F.

Remove the remaining dough ball from the fridge and allow it to sit at room temperature for a few minutes to soften.

Remove the pie plate from the fridge and pour the filling into the crust.

Roll out the remaining dough ball into a circle that is slightly larger than the pie plate, then drape it over the top of the filled crust and pinch the edges shut. Using a sharp knife, cut ½-inch slits in the top crust (this will keep the filling from overheating and "exploding").

Brush the top crust with the beaten egg.

Bake for 30 minutes, or until the crust is golden brown.

Add fresh sprigs of thyme and rosemary for garnish.

WARM, COZY, AND OPEN

Mastering the Nordic Art
of Hygge at Home

My sister, Ashlyn, lived abroad with her family in Copenhagen, Denmark, for more than a decade. During those years, I visited her there often and was always amazed at how good the Scandinavians are at creating cozy experiences. Whether they're picnicking in a big city park or cruising the canals in an electric boat or meeting up in someone's home for a birthday party, they have a unique approach to creating comfortable atmospheres that encourage the making of meaningful memories.

By now, you've probably heard of the Nordic phenomenon called hygge (pronounced "*hoo*-gah"), but for me, hygge is much more than a trend. It's part of the Scandinavian culture I *really* connect with, something I've felt intuitively but until learning about hygge never had a word for. I've always been a homebody, so when I stumbled upon the concept of hygge while visiting Ashlyn, I realized, "These people totally get me!" Extra-soft blankets; oversize outerwear; warm pastries every day; candles, cake, and cuddles. Discovering hygge helped me give a name to a specific feeling that I've appreciated and longed for my whole life. I guess I'm just a Scandi at heart!

This homebody's guide to cozy Nordic hygge is a collection of simple tips for those chilly winter months that can dial up the coziness and help us gather strength and joy from those we love the most.

SET THE STAGE

Ask any Scandinavian: hygge can happen almost anywhere and at any time—at a spring picnic, during a summer day at the beach, while picking apples in September, or while the family is gathered in close around a Christmas dinner. But there are certain ways to help hygge come to life. Below is a short list of some general elements that set the stage for a hyggelig (pronounced "*hoo*-gah-lee," meaning "hygge-like") experience.

Warmth is always important, whether that means wrapping up in a woolly blanket on the sofa or sitting at a sunny café table or snuggling with a loved one.

Lighting helps set a mood: all-natural candles (see October), tasteful twinkle lights, a fire in the fireplace, strategically placed lamps that aren't too bright and aren't directly overhead—all these allow people to relax and settle into a comfy gathering.

Try to create **spaces for pairs and small groups to sit together** and chat. Chairs that face each other, pillows and blankets on the floor, picnic blankets on the grass, and a bench in the sun can encourage the kind of face-to-face and shoulder-to-shoulder intimacy that jumpstarts a great convo.

Quiet music in the background can really tie the whole thing together. The choice of music depends on the occasion, but in general, keep it mellow so that it doesn't overpower the conversations in the room. The music should be a natural part of the atmosphere, not a focal point.

DON'T STRESS

The core of any hyggelig experience is a stress-free vibe. So if there are things in your life or space that might cause anxiety, they have to go. Whether it's your cell phone or your computer or that pile of clutter in the corner or the TV news droning on in the other room, make sure those things are turned off, put away, and out of sight. As we all know, stress can also be caused by people in our lives, so be thoughtful about whom you invite to any occasion or place that you hope will be hyggelig. This isn't about excluding anyone: it's about protecting certain moments that you hope will be calm, intimate, and life-giving.

SLOW DOWN

Hygge is all about being fully present in the moment—this moment—right now. This means you can't rush it. You can't hurry in or hurry out or "squeeze it in" between other activities or obligations on a busy Sunday. Hygge tends to happen organically when we make space for genuine connection in our lives but don't overprogram or put undue pressure on any given gathering. The ingredients for a truly hyggelig occasion are simple: relaxation, good conversation, nice food and drink, and reconnection. They can't be forced into existence; they need time and room to breathe. So when it comes to creating a hyggelig experience, it's important to slow down and just be in the moment.

PREPARE TO SHARE

A big part of hygge is togetherness—gathering with others to share an evening or a long brunch. And the point of coming together is to connect, right? To look each other in the eyes, to catch up on what's been happening, to tell stories and jokes, to rekindle friendships. In order for this to work, we all have to participate; we all have to bring something to the table, both literally and figuratively.

This can take a lot of forms. Of course, if I'm the host, then I'm sharing my home. If I'm a guest, I always bring something along to share—flowers or wine or fresh bread or a cake if I have time to make one. But whenever we gather with friends, we also bring news from our lives, our joys and successes as well as our sorrows and defeats. So any gathering that is truly in the spirit of hygge will also have a sense of safety. People will feel free to share food and laughs as well as be real with each other and speak from the heart, without judgment. This is how genuine connections are made. This is how hygge comes to life.

STAY OPEN TO SAYING YES

Finally, you will need to prepare *yourself*. When a gathering reaches "peak hygge," an organic evolution of energy takes place. What was once an evening on the patio can easily turn into a rowdy romp in the pool. What was originally meant to be a night of wine and cheese by the fireplace suddenly turns into an epic game of hilarious charades. What started as a lovely picnic in the park turns into a spontaneous road trip to the beach. I've seen it happen. I've done it myself. And you know what? It's so special when a truly hyggelig gathering morphs into something fun and carefree.

True, it's not always natural for me to embrace this sort of freedom. So I have to consciously remember to stay openhearted and open-minded. But if I can, I love to say yes to the silly and spontaneous experiences that spring up when people gather together. And that's half the beauty of a truly hyggelig gathering: they usually inspire more gatherings . . . sometimes the next weekend, sometimes the next month. If you're feeling especially connected, sometimes the gathering just keeps carrying on into the wee hours . . . or the next morning or afternoon!

HEALTHIER BAKED APPLE CRISP

*This yummy, gluten-free spin on classic apple crisp is sweet enough to
serve as a dessert and healthy enough to serve as a warm winter breakfast.*

While there are tons of delightful apple-based foods that I enjoy every fall, apple crisp is my very favorite. It's so simple, but it also has an amazing combination of textures and flavors. There's the warm, tart apples swimming in a wonderful cinnamon sauce, the crispy, nutty shell of baked goodness on top, and of course, you have to have vanilla ice cream on the side to balance the whole thing and tie it together. I mean, what's not to love?

This healthy, gluten-free variation of the classic retains all the essential elements: oats, nuts, cinnamon, butter, and plenty of apples. I love that you can easily modify this recipe for your friends' or family members' dietary needs: for example, it can be made gluten free, dairy free, and nut free. Plus, you can bake it in a single baking dish or in ramekins for cute individual servings. And since it's not as indulgent as other crisps, I love to eat it for breakfast on a cold winter morning; I just add a scoop of Greek yogurt on the side.

I'm sure you'll love each and every morsel of this crisp's warm, gooey, cinnamony, appley goodness. And don't forget a big cup of coffee—that's essential. It's all you need for a perfect November moment!

PREP TIME: 10 MINUTES

COOK TIME: 45 TO 60 MINUTES

TOTAL TIME: 70 MINUTES

SERVES 6 TO 8

FOR THE TOPPING

⅔ cup almond flour

⅓ cup firmly packed coconut sugar

½ cup chopped raw unsalted pecans

⅓ cup rolled oats

¼ teaspoon ground cinnamon

¼ cup (½ stick) unsalted butter, melted, or ¼ cup coconut oil

FOR THE FILLING

6 medium Granny Smith apples, peeled and cut into ½-inch cubes

¼ cup maple syrup

1 teaspoon ground cinnamon

1 teaspoon vanilla extract

FOR SERVING

Vanilla-bean ice cream or Greek yogurt

TO MAKE THE TOPPING

In a large bowl, combine the flour, sugar, pecans, oats, and cinnamon.

Pour in the melted butter and use your hands to blend until the mixture becomes crumbly and resembles wet sand. Cover the bowl with plastic wrap and set aside.

TO MAKE THE FILLING

Preheat the oven to 350°F.

Generously grease an 8 × 8-inch baking pan.

Combine the apples, maple syrup, cinnamon, and vanilla in a large bowl and toss to combine.

Scoop out ⅓ cup of the topping mixture and toss it with the apple mixture.

Transfer the apple mixture to the baking pan and cover evenly with the remaining topping.

Bake the crisp for 45 to 60 minutes, or until the topping is golden brown and the filling is bubbling.

Remove the crisp from the oven. Place the pan on a wire rack and allow to cool for 10 minutes.

Serve warm with your favorite ice cream or Greek yogurt.

DECEMBER

A SEASON OF CONTENTMENT

I LOVE CHRISTMASTIME.

My parents did an amazing job of making Christmas magical for my sister and me when we were little; they worked hard and made thoughtful choices and filled our house with enchanted stories, delicious food that we only enjoyed around the holidays, and fun traditions.

My first favorite tradition was making cookies for Santa on Christmas Eve. These cookies had to be made the exact same way—the right way—every year. Santa was counting on us, after all. First, we would smoosh together two regular-size slice-and-bake cookie dough slabs to make jumbo-size cookies. As soon as they came out of the oven, we would carefully press M&M's—only green and red M&M's, mind you—into the warm top of the fresh cookies. The golden creations were incredible, amazing, perfect. And we wanted to eat them all. But these cookies weren't for us—they were for Santa. He would be expecting them. So we restrained ourselves.

Then, just before bed, we would arrange these buttery masterpieces on a special Christmas plate and place them by the fireplace—in the exact same spot as the previous year—with a big glass of cold milk. Then my sister and I would scurry off to bed, where we would fall asleep, carefully listening for the sound of sleigh bells.

The second tradition was also about sharing treats with Christmas guests. This time, though, the snacks were for our furry flying guests. That's right: Santa's reindeer—Comet and Cupid and the whole gang.

Every year on Christmas Eve Day, my dad climbed up on top of the house and emptied full bags of cornflakes onto the roof. I now know this must have looked totally insane to the neighbors, but for our family, this was essential Christmas work. A job that had to be done. If the reindeer were going to fly all the way around the world in one night, then they needed sugar and carbs and fiber to make it. That's just basic nutrition science, people! Anyway, thanks to our dad, Santa and the team knew they could always count on us to help them fuel up for the night's big journey.

It's worth noting that there was always a second part to this tradition . . . at some point on Christmas Day, usually an hour or so after we had finished opening presents, my dad would drain a cup of coffee and say (in all seriousness), "Well, I better go up and take care of the mess on the roof." By this he didn't mean the thousands of flakes of breakfast cereal he had poured out the day before: he meant mess, as in reindeer mess. And so year after year, in our robes and slippers, my sister and I would stand in the driveway on Christmas Day, watching our dad shuffle around on the roof, making a big deal of all the Dasher droppings and Prancer poo. "Oh, wow—it's a lot more than last year," he'd say. "They must be extra healthy. It's probably all the fiber in those cornflakes." Again, I can only imagine what the neighbors thought. But for us, this was an important tradition, part of the magic tapestry of Christmas that our parents wove each year.

I will forever be grateful to my mom and dad for making those childhood Christmases so special. But as I look back, one thing stands out very clearly: Christmas was about the family patterns that were established over time, those whimsical, imaginative traditions that helped shape my perception of the holiday—and of life itself—many of which I still enjoy today and plan to carry on with my own children.

In our care, traditions become our own, and then, when we pass them on, they become something else for our children and grandchildren. This is how they live on, generation after generation. Come to think of it, maybe this is a big reason why Christmas is so enchanting for kids of all ages: because many of the traditions come down

to us from an ancient past that is both mysterious and magical. But no matter where our special winter rituals come from, the thing that unites them is the emphasis on togetherness. The heart and soul of this special season is about connecting with others.

Now that I have a child of my own, the magic of Christmas has a new glow about it. Something just happens when you get the chance to introduce a sweet little human to a Christmas tree covered in tiny white lights, a morning of fresh snow, and the chaotic frenzy of unwrapping presents. It's more than just fun; it's pure delight.

Marcus and I both want to pass on our love for the magic of the Christmas season and the unique beauty of winter to our kids. Even though James is little, we're following our parents' example by investing in special traditions that he can enjoy now and look forward to for years to come. For our family, this means prioritizing people above presents and quality time together above toys and treats. We know it won't always be easy (what kid on the planet doesn't love toys and treats?), but this is our goal: center Christmastime on gratitude for the gift of another year of life and the simple joys that come from being together.

This can and will look different from year to year as our kids grow up. And sure, we're going to be making up a lot of it as we go, especially as we get to know who our kids are as individuals and what specific aspects of the season light up their imaginations. But I imagine our future Christmases will include quite a bit of family baking, board games spread out on the floor beside the fireplace, long family walks in the woods, and lessons on how to properly build a fire, choose the "perfect" Christmas tree, and, of course, make Santa's all-time favorite cookies—you know, the extra-large ones with red and green M&M's pressed carefully into the top. Will our family leave food up on the roof for Rudolph and his pals every Christmas Eve? I think I'll leave that one up to Marcus. Who knows? Maybe James will even pass some of these traditions on to our grandchildren someday.

Ultimately, my hope is that, regardless of the pageantry of the season, December will always be a season of quiet contentment and a time for gratitude, joy, and reflection. A season with people at the center. A season defined by shared experiences. A season that inspires both nostalgia for old memories and a willingness to make new ones. A time both to remember and to look ahead to the future.

December is always the last page on a calendar, the final chapter before we ring in a new year. But we know intuitively that this isn't the whole story. December is not the period at the end of a sentence. It's more like a comma, a chance to pause and take a breath, to look both ways, backward and forward, to the past and to the future. A season to express gratitude for what has happened and how we have struggled and grown and changed. It is also a chance to look forward in hope at what could evolve in the days and months and seasons ahead.

And so here in the heart of winter, we wait for the return of the sun. We wait for the ground to soften and the earth to warm. But at the same time, change is stirring, growth is happening. Another calendar year may be finished. But I am not. And neither are you.

CHRISTMAS MORNING
SOURDOUGH CINNAMON ROLLS

These big, soft, fluffy rolls, both comforting and complex, are one of my
all-time favorite sweet treats, a gift that just keeps on giving!

One of the many joys of working with sourdough and sourdough starters at home is that you can make all kinds of delicious things beyond the basic bread loaf. Sourdough cinnamon rolls are the most deliciously decadent thing I have ever made from my starter. One of our family traditions is to bake these rolls on Christmas morning (I do all the prep the day before, which makes Christmas much more relaxing), serving them fresh and warm in the late morning, when the initial whirlwind and excitement of the day have calmed down a bit. Trust me: it's not the gifts wrapped in bright paper and tidy twine but the gift of big, fluffy, gooey, melt-in-your-mouth sourdough cinnamon rolls that is the true Christmas morning miracle.

PREP TIME: 16 HOURS, INCLUDING TIME FOR THE DOUGH TO RISE

COOK TIME: 25 TO 30 MINUTES

TOTAL TIME: 16½ HOURS

SERVES 8

FOR THE DOUGH

⅔ cup whole milk

½ cup (1 stick) unsalted butter, melted, plus more for coating the bowl

1 large egg

½ cup (100 grams) bubbly, active sourdough starter (page 19)

2 tablespoons granulated sugar

3 cups all-purpose flour, plus extra for dusting work surfaces

1 teaspoon fine sea salt

Neutral oil, for the work surface

FOR THE FILLING

½ cup (1 stick) salted butter, at room temperature

1 cup firmly packed light brown sugar

2 tablespoons ground cinnamon

½ cup heavy cream

FOR THE FROSTING

6 ounces cream cheese, at room temperature

⅓ cup (5⅓ tablespoons) butter, at room temperature

1 cup confectioners' sugar, or more to taste

½ tablespoon vanilla extract

¼ teaspoon fine sea salt

STEP 1: MAKE THE DOUGH

The day before you plan to serve the rolls, combine the milk and melted butter in a small bowl. Allow the mixture to cool before using.

Combine the egg, sourdough starter, and sugar in the bowl of a stand mixer fitted with the paddle attachment. Mix on medium speed to combine.

Reduce the speed to low and gradually pour in the milk mixture.

Add the flour and salt.

Continue mixing until a rough, sticky dough forms, about 1 minute.

Scrape down the sides of the bowl. Cover with a damp tea towel and let rest for 30 minutes.

After the dough has rested, switch to the dough hook attachment. Knead on medium-low speed for 6 to 8 minutes. The dough should feel soft and pull away from the sides of the bowl when it's ready. If it's too sticky, you can add a small amount of flour.

STEP 2: LET THE DOUGH RISE OVERNIGHT

Lightly butter a large bowl and transfer the dough to the bowl. The dough needs plenty of room to expand while it rises. Cover with plastic wrap and let rise for 1 hour.

Stretch and fold the dough: grab a portion of the dough from the side of the bowl and stretch it upward. Fold it over toward the center of the bowl. Give the bowl a quarter turn, then stretch and fold the dough again. Repeat until all the dough has been stretched and folded over.

Cover the dough with a damp tea towel and let the dough rise overnight until it has doubled in size, about 8 to 12 hours or more, in a warm spot (I like to put it in the oven, with the heat turned off but with the light on).

STEP 3: ROLL OUT THE DOUGH

The next morning, line a 9 x 13-inch pan with parchment paper.

Lightly oil and flour your work surface to prevent sticking. Coax the risen dough out of the bowl and gently pat it into a rough rectangle on the work surface.

Let the dough rest in this shape for 10 minutes, for easier rolling.

Dust the dough and your rolling pin with flour. Roll out the dough into a roughly 16 x 12-inch rectangle. Set aside while you make the filling.

STEP 4: MAKE THE FILLING

In a medium bowl, combine the butter, brown sugar, and cinnamon. Mix until well combined.

Using an offset spatula, spread the filling evenly over the dough, leaving a ½-inch border around the edges.

STEP 5: SHAPE AND CUT THE DOUGH

Starting on the long side (the 16-inch side), roll the dough tightly into a log, pressing down gently as you go. The log needs to be tight so the cinnamon swirls stay nicely intact. You should end with the seam of the log facing down.

⟶

Using a sharp knife or bench scraper, cut the log crosswise into 2-inch sections. (Before cutting, I like to lightly score the dough to make sure each piece is roughly the same size.)

Flip the cut rolls so that the swirls are facing up and place them into the prepared pan. Let rest for 1 to 2 hours, or until the dough puffs up. This is the time to freeze some or all of the rolls if you want to bake and serve them later.

STEP 6: BAKE THE ROLLS

Preheat the oven to 350°F.

Pour the heavy cream over the top of the risen rolls, allowing it to soak in and pool around the rolls.

Place the pan on the center rack of the oven and bake for 30 to 40 minutes, or until the rolls are light golden brown.

Remove from the oven and allow to cool in the pan for 10 to 15 minutes.

STEP 7: MAKE THE FROSTING

While the rolls are resting, combine the cream cheese and butter in a large bowl. Blend with a hand mixer until creamy and smooth. Add the sugar, vanilla, and salt. Mix until fully combined.

When ready to serve, spread the frosting over the rolls in the pan.

Plate, celebrate, share, and enjoy this delightful and decadent achievement.

SYMBOLS OF LOVE

Creative Ideas for
Meaningful Gifting

The holiday season is fun, but it can also be super stressful. To combat the stress of gift giving during the holidays, Marcus and I employ a strategy that helps us keep things in perspective.

First, whenever I can simplify things during the holidays, I do. If that means hosting a potluck or ordering takeout instead of spending two days in the kitchen, I'm all for that. If we have to say no to more holiday gatherings than we say yes to in order to stay centered, that's what we do. Also, if we have to choose between spending money on a shared experience versus spending money on stuff, we go for the experience every time. And lastly, as far as gifts are concerned, simplicity is always the goal.

For our family, less really is more when it comes to Christmas gifts. When we give, we try to make creativity and originality a big part of the process. That might mean searching vintage shops for quirky items or buying something we can share or even making a gift we know others will enjoy. Whenever something is handcrafted, that always adds an extra layer of beauty and thoughtfulness. Honestly, a meaningful holiday gift can be anything: a jar of sourdough starter that promises many tasty treats to come, a framed bouquet of wildflowers to remind us of the warmth of summer, a set of hand-dyed tea towels, or a lovingly propagated monstera in a pretty vintage pot.

But whether we buy the gifts we give or make them with our hands, the true beauty of any gift is what it communicates between the giver

and recipient. Gift giving is such a personal and intentional act: it demonstrates what you know and how you feel about the person you're giving to.

I've also found you can convey this through the wrapping as well. So below are some of my favorite ways to wrap gifts with imagination and care.

THREE THINGS THAT MAKE GIFT WRAPPING A LITTLE MORE SPECIAL AND A BIT MORE BEAUTIFUL...

1. Use double-sided tape! Seems like a no-brainer, but it gives the gift an all-around cleaner, neater feel, and it often holds better than single-sided tape.

2. Using natural elements such as dried orange slices and fir branches adds a lot to your gift presentation, both visually and aromatically.

3. Use items you already have in your house, such as little gold bells from other Christmas decorations and colorful fabric scraps. You could even wrap a gift in a towel or blanket intended to be part of the gift.

CECE'S FAMOUS CAJUN GUMBO

Preparing authentic, homemade gumbo with a lot of love is a family tradition I inherited from my mom. No matter where I live or what is going on in my life, this deeply comforting recipe helps connect me with my childhood, my family, and especially my sweet mama.

Gumbo is my mom's love language. This is her signature dish, especially in the wintertime and around the holidays, when everyone is gathered together. We all love it—my dad, me, my sister, our husbands. Even the grandkids ask her to make it when we're all together. "Please, CeCe," they plead ever so sweetly. "Please make gumbo for us!" (We let the kiddos ask, but we are all thinking the same thing.) She sometimes pretends to be put out by the hassle, but we know the truth: she lives for this.

Anytime Mom makes gumbo, it is an all-day event. The family eats a basic breakfast and makes sure to exercise a lot that day. Sometimes we even skip lunch so that we are extra hungry by dinnertime. Meanwhile, watching my mom work in the kitchen and seeing her beautiful gumbo come together, step by meticulous, patient step, is always fun. She puts so much care into the whole process. She always has. All afternoon, our anticipation and hunger are building while the house fills up with an amazing, rich fragrance. "When will it be ready?" we ask. The answer is always the same: "It will be ready when it's ready."

To be honest, I'm not sure if Mom knows exactly where her famous recipe originated, but she has made it so many times by now that it's all basically muscle memory. For us, though, every bowl of CeCe's gumbo is a kind of culinary magic that never disappoints. I know I'm lucky to have a mom who is so gifted in the kitchen and who is so willing to share her tips and tricks with me. Over the years, I've tried to follow in her footsteps. And while my pots of gumbo are always a hit (I follow Mom's recipe every time), they're never quite as rich or comforting as hers.

I hope you give this recipe a try and share it with someone you love. Maybe it will become a special holiday tradition in your family—nothing would make my sweet mama happier.

PREP TIME: 30 MINUTES

COOK TIME: 3 HOURS

TOTAL TIME: 3½ HOURS

SERVES 6 TO 8

6 to 8 cups chicken stock (not chicken broth)

12 ounces andouille, kielbasa, or other smoked sausage, sliced into coins

1 cup all-purpose flour, plus more if necessary

1 cup vegetable oil, plus more if necessary

1 bunch of celery with leaves (about 5 stalks), diced

1 green bell pepper, diced

1 large yellow onion, diced

4 scallions, sliced

½ cup fresh parsley leaves, finely chopped

2 to 3 cloves garlic, minced

1 to 2 tablespoons CeCe's Cajun Seasoning (page 47) or prepared Cajun seasoning

Meat from a 4- to 5-pound roast chicken or rotisserie chicken, shredded

1 pound raw shrimp, peeled and cleaned (optional)

STEP 1: HEAT THE STOCK AND BROWN THE SAUSAGE

Pour the chicken stock into a large soup pot. This will become your gumbo pot. Bring to a simmer over medium heat.

Arrange the sausage in a single layer in a large skillet and cook over medium-high heat. Brown sausage well on one side, 2 to 3 minutes. Using a fork or tongs, flip each slice over so that each piece gets nice and brown on both sides.

Remove the sausage from the skillet and set aside.

STEP 2: MAKE THE ROUX

In the same skillet, combine the flour and oil.

Cook over medium-low heat, stirring constantly, for 30 to 45 minutes. Do not walk away from the stove while the roux is cooking. The roux is finished when it turns a chocolate-brown color and has a soft but thick cookie dough–like consistency. Add more flour or oil as needed to reach this consistency.

STEP 3: COOK THE VEGETABLES

Once the roux is ready, add the celery, bell pepper, onions, scallions, parsley, and garlic to the skillet.

Add the Cajun seasoning and stir to combine.

Cook until the veggies are soft, about 10 minutes.

Ladle 2 cups of hot chicken stock from your gumbo pot into a measuring cup and gradually pour it into the roux. Don't pour too fast, or the roux will get gummy.

Stir to combine, then simmer for 5 minutes.

FOR SERVING

**2 cups cooked white rice
for serving**

Hot sauce of choice

**Crusty French bread,
lightly toasted and
buttered**

STEP 4: COMBINE, SIMMER, SAMPLE, AND SERVE

Transfer the vegetable mixture to the pot where the remainder of the stock is simmering.

Add the chicken and sausage. Simmer over low heat for at least 1 hour.

Taste the gumbo and adjust the seasonings to suit your taste. Once you feel that you've achieved perfection, add the shrimp, if desired.

Simmer over low heat for another 5 minutes, or until the shrimp are fully cooked.

Serve the gumbo warm over rice with a dash of your favorite Louisiana hot sauce. My mom and dad love to have a big chunk of buttered French bread with their gumbo. This is a very good idea, I must say. Enjoy!

REFLECTION

Where and when do you feel most content—at home, in nature, near the sea, while working, or while spending time with family? Consider why these people and places make you feel so at peace. Is it a sense of security? Beauty? Purpose? Belonging? Maybe it is all these things and more. But whatever the reasons, identifying—and naming—those things that make us most content can be a helpful way to grow in our understanding of ourselves, our world, and one another.

CONCLUSION

This Is How We Grow

We will likely never accomplish all that we want to do in a single year.

We will never be able to do it all, never experience or learn or become everything we had hoped or planned. And that's okay. It really is. Every year of life is a gift, a chance to face changes and challenges and grow through these experiences in our own ways. Whether it's the challenge of moving to a new location, starting a new relationship or ending one, having a baby, navigating friendships near and far, or weathering an injury or illness, you have what it takes to face it. There will be ups and downs, but the only way onward is forward.

Wherever we are in our lives, wherever we are in the world or in the cycle of the year, there is always room for growth. You are not finished—none of us is. We will continue to change and grow. That's the great gift of life—the chance to continue, to experience another spring, summer, fall, and winter. It is a chance to press on, to keep reaching upward, up from wherever we are right now, up toward the light.

Is it hard at times? Yes. But it's also hopeful. None of us knows what the next season of life or the next year or decade will hold for us. But we have come this far. All of us have overcome obstacles, experienced joy, and changed in innumerable ways over the years. We aren't who we once were. And we do not know exactly who we will someday become. But we have today. We have right now.

There is still much more to be done. More challenges. More change. More growth. More life. Perhaps the best we can do is celebrate each and every season of life—the planting, the waiting, and the harvesting. And so we embrace life, come what may.

I believe this is how we become fully alive. This is how we come to know our true selves and understand others. This is how we grow, day by day and season by season. Rooted in love, nourished by hope, and reaching always for the light.